07/09/02

SANDY, STAY IN THE GAME
WITH ME — TAKE CARE OF
YOURSELF — STAY WELL,

Don W. Ray

Still in the Game

by
Don W. Ray

Bridgewood Press
Phoenix, Arizona

Acknowledgments

Appreciation goes to the strangers and near-strangers who gave of themselves to me in times of need. As a diabetic, I have many times been needy over the years. Somewhere on Cleveland's East Side there was a paper boy that gave me candy when I needed it desperately. You're a big kid now, but I thank you just the same.

Appreciation goes to those I have known for a lifetime. Without my family, this book never would have been possible. I wouldn't be here. To the youngsters that were there for me to coach in baseball, basketball and football, you are a very important part of this book. Each of you, in some way, added to the pleasures I have had as a coach. For that, I am grateful. My teammates for a long period of time were instrumental in helping me be a better one. There are too many to mention, but I feel certain that each of them will know who they are. Thanks, guys. You sure did make my life a happy one. I refer to friends often within the following chapters and will not ever be able to express the importance, the value they have given me over the years. Some have made statements entered in this book, but others all so special to me are here, as well. Their names are scattered between the lines of many pages.

So important in this publication has been the input, editing and guidance of my sister Donna and her husband, Michel. The positive motivation and early typing generated by my daughter Sheila cannot go unacknowledged. It would have been impossible to bring this book together without you three.

Donnalee Sarda, Editor

Library of Congress Cataloging in Publication Data

Ray, Don W., 1934-
    Still in the game : the story of sports, sugar diabetes, and me: 67 years in the making / by Don W. Ray.
        p. cm.
Includes index
    ISBN 0-927015-28-5 (pbk.)
    1. Ray, Don W., 1934- 2. Athletes—United States—Biography
3. Athletes with disabilities—United States—Biography. 4. Diabetics—United States—Biography. l. Title.
    GV697.R39 A3 2001
    796'.092—dc21

                                    2001008671

Printed in the United States of America

Dedication

To Penny for her unfailing love as my wife,
  a mother and grandmother
To Mom and Dad and sisters Gerri and Donna
To my children Dawn, Sheila, Debby and Scott
To my angel Eileen
To my doctor, Henry H. Roenigk Sr.

TABLE OF CONTENTS

Foreword

Still in the Game provides insight into an invaluable experience, that of a pioneer in living with Type 1, "juvenile" diabetes. Don W. Ray has lived with *diabetes mellitus* for more than six decades. Insulin to treat the disease became widely used only ten years prior to his needing it. Ray's parents were pioneers as well, as information on the disease was limited and testing and treatment methods were primitive. Myths and misinformation circulated. Don's parents had no way to know then that their son would live a long and successful life.

Today, parents of diabetics can look at Don and others and know that through managed care their children, too, can thrive and prosper. However, it is ultimately left up to the patient to manage the disorder on a daily and hourly basis. This is where the "can do" attitude of Don Ray provides a way. Perhaps he inherited his spirit from his dedicated parents, or perhaps from my father, Dr. Henry H. Roenigk, Senior, the Ray's family physician during Don's critical adolescent years, and who saved his life from a diabetic coma.

Not only was my father Don's physician, but "Little Ray" and I played high school basketball together before Don was ousted from the team because the school physician feared his diabetes. I didn't know then that "Little Ray" had diabetes. I think Don liked it that way. He wanted to be like every other kid — to be in sports, enjoy other friends and not feel held back by his disease.

He has lived his life like that.

It is now fifty years later that, through this book, Don and I will meet again, this time with our families.

Having not seen each other in 50 years, Don Ray (right) the smallest player on the team, and Henry H. Roenigk, Jr., the tallest (left), pictured here at John Marshall High School, are reunited through the publication of *Still in the Game*. Henry's father, Dr. Henry H. Roenigk, Sr. was Don's family physician and was attributed with saving Don's life from a diabetic coma — just months before this 1949 photo was taken.

Actually, our paths almost crossed on many occasions that we were not aware of: at Ohio University, and at Cleveland Clinic when Don was a patient after a serious auto accident and at which I was Chairman of Dermatology. We share a love for the Cleveland Indians and the Cleveland Browns, attended countless games, and we both agree that Jim Brown is the greatest football player ever. I am honored to find that Don still considers my father to be one of the most important people in his life.

My granddaughter Katie Roenigk read this book prior to publication. Her comments are found in the

Afterword section. She said the book held more for her than information about baseball or diabetes. She said she found a man's philosophy of life to take what was given and to make the best of it. Don certainly did that. To both Katie and me, "Still in the Game" means, among other things, still alive.

This book provides a welcome perspective and solid advice for not only those suffering from this disease, but for anyone interested in creating positive lifestyles and attitudes. Don's Diabetic Rules are a good prescription for anyone, even if you don't have diabetes.

As a physician I have witnessed that even those with illness and disease can "give it all they've got," and in so doing, participate in almost everything they find meaningful. Personally, I have had open heart surgery and a broken neck but have been able to continue fully practicing my medical profession. I'm still in active private practice.

Now aware of Don Ray's outlook on life, I can add that I too am *still in the game*!

Henry H. Roenigk, Jr., M.D.

Dr. Henry H. Roenigk, Jr., is in private practice in Phoenix, AZ with Arizona Advanced Dermatology. He was a professor and Chairman of Dermatology at Cleveland Clinic for ten years before joining the faculty of Northwestern University Medical School. From 1977 to 1997 he was a professor and Chairman of Dermatology. He is the son of the Ray family's physician mentioned in this book.

A Personal Preface

At each chapter throughout this book I have included a little "one liner" that I refer to as "bits and pieces." I have always been a fan of these clever and often motivational comments. I have used them when coaching, when a speaking opportunity presented itself, or just in a one-on-one conversation with a friend or acquaintance. The bits and pieces have been compiled from books, magazines and from the radio. I usually cannot provide the author, but I thank the originator of these short comments.

Here are the "Bits and Pieces" I have enjoyed that did not make it into a chapter subheading:

When geese fly in formation, they fly 80% faster.

When you get to the end of your rope, tie a knot and hang on.

Class is an intangible thing but it always shows.

When one door closes another opens. Don't spend much time looking at the closed door for you might not see the one that is opening.

Everyone has tough days but that is only to make you a better person.

Success comes in cans, not in cannots.

You have to work for everything that is worthwhile.

If you don't stand for something, you might fall for anything.

It takes courage to stand by your convictions when so many of those around us have no convictions at all.

Babies are a great way to start people.

And I've added a poem of my own about diabetes.

The Sugar Man

I think of the Engine that thought it could
I think of the young boy who thought he should.
Somebody once said that it couldn't be done
But of that silly statement, he would have none.

Deep down inside he knew he was right
And to argue this point could start a fight.
To accomplish these things he followed a guide,
Listened alertly and took all in stride.

"Cannot" for him, a word hard to find
As he wouldn't let that word enter his mind.
Follow this lead: do the best that you can
And you too can enjoy being The Sugar Man.

DWR

1
Sugar and Me

Life is an ongoing project.

Anonymous

I freed my right arm from his grip and proceeded to punch Jim right smack dab in the middle of his forehead. My gold ring left my initials prominently outlined on his face for a week. Kelly and Jim could laugh with me about it afterwards, but there was no humor at the time.

There was another incident at my apartment that proved to be an embarrassment to Kelly, who prided himself in his strength. He was strong! On that day, Kelly sat in bed with me, propped me up and put a huge bear hug on me while Jim proceeded to put sugared orange juice into my mouth. But I was stronger than the beefy Irishman. Don't ask me why, but for some reason, probably known to medical people, when having an insulin reaction, a "wing-ding" I call it, diabetics often seem to gain strength that we normally wouldn't have. Kelly and Jim remarked to me how noticeably different the increase in my strength was.

For years, when I would see these two police officers elsewhere in the neighborhood, we'd acknowledge each other. It was always a pleasure to see them pass by in their squad car. Jim continued for years to kid Kelly that I, this "little guy," broke his grip. And Kelly would not let an opportunity go by when he could tease Jim about my initials being imprinted on his forehead. I'm grateful it was they who were called to help me out of my low blood sugar episodes. I'm grateful they understood that although they tried to help me, my unconscious condition during the "wing-dings" did not allow me to cooperate. I do not recall Jim's last name, or Kelly's first name, but if they have an opportunity to read this book, they'll know who they are. By the way, you two, thank you very much.

My 'Problem'

Diabetes really never changed my life —
it helped me to lead a better one. DWR

During those years in my late teens and early twenties, word spread through my friends and teammates that I was having "problems." Certainly my Mom had something to do with enlightening my buddies and their parents about my "condition," because suddenly I was invited to their homes for dinner.

"Don, this Sunday we're having pasta, come on over," said the Pujolas family. During high school and for my first year at Ohio University, my closest friend was Bob Pujolas. Pop Pujolas, a big man of about 285 pounds, often said to me, "I just love to watch you eat." Spaghetti-night Sundays helped me eat my way toward my 6,000 calorie a day diet. Sometimes after a game, I'd stop at the Fergusons. Pa Fergy coached baseball and through him I met their son Howie, a mighty fine athlete.

Another perk to my "problem" was the standing invitation to the Krause household for a dinner "date" every Tuesday. Fred Krause and I played baseball, football and basketball together since our teen years. Fred may have been the only athlete I ever played with in those early years that could have made the National Football League. Tuesday dinners were such a good time that I didn't miss many. After dinner we and his parents would get comfortable in their living room and watch "Cheyenne Bodie," the escapades of a tall cowboy hero played by actor Clint Walker, the idol of millions of fans.

At any rate, the "problem" that I was having was sugar diabetes, and I had already had it for more than fifteen years.

Fred Krause, Howie Ferguson and I were the three musketeers. We double and triple-dated, and eventually were in each other's weddings. Years later, Fred and Marcie and Penny and I would celebrate our 40-something wedding anniversaries together. Howie Ferguson died of a heart attack while playing volley ball at the age of 52, but not before becoming a legend as a wrestling coach and an extremely successful businessman. He had been in the peak of good health. No one can predict the future — I was the one who was told I might not live to be 50.

I met Don Ray in 1950 when we played sports in city parks and on our own hand-made baseball fields. Don, a few years my senior, was instrumental in teaching me the competitiveness of sports that has impacted all phases of my life. He's been a loyal friend to me for fifty years.

My strongest recollection of Don is his love of the game. In spite of his diabetes, his sheer self-

discipline and perseverance always amazed me. He wanted to play so badly that being a diabetic was not going to stop him. Anything with a ball, Don played. Whether watching him or participating with him, I was aware that Don could deplete his sugar and his body could react by going into what Don called a "wing-ding." Since Don always gave 100% of his energy, he required more sugar to maintain a balanced level. There were times Don would deny that his sugar level was low, and it was difficult convincing him that he needed sugar. Fortunately, he would relent and take my and our teammates' advice to drink something sweet.

I also saw Don on social occasions when our friends thought that alcohol was needed to have a good time. This was not true for Don. He always joined the social functions, without being able to drink, yet used his sense of humor to create a good time for himself and those around him.

I never saw Don's life limited because of his diabetes. He learned about the illness and from an early age worked at controlling his condition.

Fred Krause

2
When it began

A smooth sea never made a skillful sailor. Hubert Humphrey

At first they thought I was kidding. We all knew something was wrong as we drove from Cleveland, Ohio to Pittsburgh, Pennsylvania, the site of Dad's new "transfer" job. It seemed as if every ten minutes I was extremely thirsty and had to urinate. An almost-five-year old can be bothersome on a road trip, but my frequent "bathroom breaks" were starting to get on my parents' nerves. When a convenient toilet was not available, I had to use a wayward location in a field along the highway. I had no history of this kind of problem, though I might have begun to urinate and drink more than usual about a week before the trip. Soon it was very evident that this was no playful prank. Something was wrong.

When we arrived in Clariton Village, a suburb of Pittsburgh, we settled into our new home, totally strange to me, but because I was with my family, I knew everything would be okay. My sister Gerri, although only two years older than I, was as concerned as my parents — what was wrong with Donny?

We knew no one in the new city, yet alone a good doctor. Mom asked the neighbors for referrals and we visited a physician who did a painful job of sticking needles in me to take a lot of my blood. I know very well, now, that he was doing what needed to be done, but at the time, he was not one of my favorite people. There was much conversation between Mom, Dad and the doctor, as if I wasn't there.

It was agreed that I would go to Children's Hospital in Pittsburgh for further evaluation. I'm not sure what procedure the doctor followed, but do know that he announced, after more examinations and blood work, that I had Sugar Diabetes, later called Juvenile or Type 1 diabetes. He explained to my parents that my pancreas had stopped producing insulin, a hormone that helps the body process carbohydrates. I would now need to inject insulin into my body several times a day for the rest of my life. Insulin had been discovered a mere 17 years earlier, and not marketed until 1926, 13 years before I needed it. We learned that an early warning-sign of diabetes included extreme thirst and frequency of urination. My parents were told that I would probably have a "short life span," and that this condition was hereditary, but that it "skipped a generation." This meant that my children would probably not get diabetes, but their children could. Mom and Dad explained to my sister that she would probably not get it, but that her children could.

The belief that diabetes "skips a generation" persisted for decades. It has, however, turned out to be a medical "myth." It is also untrue that diabetics will have a "short life span." I believe I can attest to that, as can others on Eli Lilly Pharmaceutical Company's registry of diabetics who have been taking insulin for more than 50 years. In my case, it's nearly 63 years.

Miraculously, Children's Hospital was one of the best hospitals in the nation for the care of juvenile diabetics. Of greater interest to me, even before age five, was the hospital's location, just down the street from Pitt Stadium where the University of Pittsburgh played football. I had already begun to take the announcement of my diabetes in stride.

For more than two weeks, I remained at the hospital. My diet was correlated to the amount of insulin prescribed so that I could lead a normal life.

Notice that I say a "normal" life, and that's exactly what I have led. My life has probably been as normal as any. I've had some bumps along the way, as I believe everybody has. I know very well that there are many, many people that have an ailment much worse than my sugar diabetes.

A Big Sister's Memories

I remember listening to my mother cry throughout many of the nights. Donny had been taken to the hospital almost immediately upon our arrival in Pittsburgh. The ward, named Rheimenschneider, was to become his temporary home. Since we wanted to be close, the rest of the family stayed in a nearby hotel. I was scared not understanding what was going on.

When Don was released from the hospital, our family life changed a little as we adapted to a new routine, and Mom at last stopped crying. Instead, she became active on behalf of her son. She went to school to meet with the administrators and each teacher to explain his needs, and that he might need sugar. She provided them with sugar cubes and oranges. She became active in PTA and friendly with the principal, Miss Stroud, who was very helpful with Don. (Decades later, when a school was named in Miss Stroud's honor, Mom, then editor of an architectural magazine, insisted that the publisher include her photo along with the school photo. This and other special relationships grew from Don's diabetes.) The arrangements at school were done quietly so that the other children did not necessarily know of his special needs. He was not given special privileges, just watched over.

Mom insisted that I, as the big sister, look out for him. One day at school, as my class was walking single-file in silence through the hallway, I passed Don standing alone in a doorway. I knew he was having what I always called "a shock," an insulin reaction, but I was afraid to break the school rules and speak up. Indeed, he was having a reaction and although his teacher tended to him, he for years afterward, found many good-humored moments to remind me that I passed him by. Then, of course, there was the time I caught his finger in the car door and he lost the tip of his left ring finger. His short finger never seemed to bother him, even when he was playing ball. My brother was always playing ball. I was one of his first pupils as he taught me to hold and swing a bat. On the whole, he was easy to watch out for. As a toddler he had blonde curly hair and big eyes of blue. As a teenager he looked like Paul Newman. He still has a great big grin and is always smiling. What a guy. He's now my big brother.

Gerri

Back to the hospital. Every piece of food I ate had to be weighed on a gram scale, every glass of milk or orange juice had to be measured by ounces. I would have 90 grams of meat, 70 grams of a vegetable, 100 grams of potatoes, 50 grams of a fresh fruit and 12 ounces of milk. That would very well describe my dinner. Everything was weighed or measured.

When I went to school, my dear mother packed each lunch every day with the proper amounts of meat, bread and fruit. Even the lettuce on a sandwich was calculated into my diet. I was permitted to buy only milk at the school cafeteria. Everything I took into my mouth was prescribed, just as if it were a medicine. When out to school or to the park, I carried two individually wrapped sugar cubes in my pocket, in case an insulin reaction would set in. An insulin reaction can occur when there is a sudden drop in the level of sugar in the blood. A low sugar reaction is called a hypoglycemic reaction. To me, a "wing-ding."

In Type 1 diabetics, the insulin-producing function of the pancreas does not work as it should to regulate food intake. Since almost everything human beings eat contains carbohydrates which the body processes as sugar, blood sugar levels rise and young diabetics must inject insulin into their bodies to get their levels back to an acceptable range.

When diabetics *use* energy, however, we, like everyone, burn sugar and therefore have less need for insulin. But how much less insulin can be difficult to predict ahead of time and we can't withdraw insulin we took earlier in the day. So for balance, we will need to take extra sugar when having an insulin reaction. Telltale signs of an insulin reaction are the inability to move normally, confusion and excessive perspiration. In advanced stages, we have difficulty talking and moving with any control of our bodies. Double vision can set in. We can persistently resist people trying to assist us in getting the sugar we desperately need. Often, an increase in our strength seems to occur, although at other times we seem to be very weak. We can lose consciousness.

Back then, things were pretty basic. We didn't have any of the many conveniences we have today: No glucose tablets, no packaged glucose of any kind. To combat a reaction, we would rely on pure white or raw sugar. Whenever possible, I preferred sugar mixed with orange juice. The juice was an enhancement for quicker results in getting the sugar into my blood stream. Candy was not nearly as readily available as it is today.

The sugar cubes I carried would often be a pain in the neck because the wrapper would become worn or it would pull apart at a seam and I would find myself with a pocket full of loose sugar. Once, on a picnic with the family, I slipped out of my trousers to my bathing suit underneath. When the swim was over, I changed back into my pants and, when home, tossed my pants on my bed. Awhile later I found a zillion ants crawling all over the bed and floor. The sugar cube had become unwrapped and the raw sugar was an invitation to these zealous ants. It was a real circus to rid the room of the little pests.

Dining Out

Teaching children to count is fine, but teaching them what counts is even better. Anonymous

In those days, going out to dinner was a rarity. Rare in that there were not many restaurants to go to, and such a "night out" was costly. When that treat did present itself, my food still had to be weighed, and the gram scale would appear to be part of our family. The family night out included Mom, Dad, Sis, me and my gram scale. Oh yes, it included my insulin, already drawn in the glass syringe and carried in a sterile metal device that held the syringe and my hypodermic needle out of harm's way. It also kept them free from germs.

The injections were taken either in the car or in the men's room. The first several years, probably until I turned ten, Mom administered my shots. From then on, I injected myself two and three times each day, every day. It became a part of my life. The dosage at dinner time was of Regular insulin, and usually Dad or Gerri would go inside the restaurant to see how soon we could be seated. This information would determine if we needed to wait and take the insulin a little later, in the rest room, or if I could take the injection while in the car. When I took it in the car, it simply meant that we were going to get to eat a bit quicker.

The insulin-taking thing was much easier in warmer weather than in the colder months when long-sleeved shirts and heavy coats complicated the process. Picture this: in the cold of winter, in the car, taking off an outer coat, rolling up sweater and shirt sleeves, or at times, taking down trousers. Then, dabbing a cotton ball in a vial of alcohol, wiping an arm or leg with that cotton ball, taking the injection, wiping the area after the injection and then rolling down or pulling up, getting back into the coat and then going to eat. In the winter, we often decided to take the shot indoors.

To me the insulin was a slight misadventure, but the glaring appearance of the scale, in view for all to see, was embarrassing. Dad couldn't very well hide it, nor did he try to, or attempt to weigh with it on the floor, and so it had a prominent resting place on the table. It seemed to me that every eye in the restaurant was riveted on that white, 6" x 6" square, ten-inch tall device. Dad was quite good at estimating size portions to weight and usually he would be right on target. At home we made a game of it and when Dad would get it right, we would cheer, but at a restaurant, we made no fuss at all. When our order was placed, we requested an extra plate which would be put on the scale. My order was straight from the menu and Dad took whatever weight was necessary to meet the required diet by transferring from the dinner plate to the scale plate. Then, after weighing the plate, the scale would be adjusted back to zero so that the food weight would be accurate. Dad often said that if everyone in the family ate what I ate, we would all be remarkably healthy.

In those days, one ordered meals *a la carte*, individually from the menu. Meat, vegetables, potato choices, salads and bread were each listed separately. Beef, pork, chicken — green beans, carrots, peas — potatoes mashed or fried — lettuce with tomato or not — white or wheat. Only on occasion did a restaurant offer a soda pop. Very seldom, Dad would need to take a portion from his plate to meet a required weight for an item. I don't ever recall his taking from other than his own plate. Mom would always insist that he use some of her portions, but no, only his.

Once in awhile Dad would order vanilla ice cream for dessert, and then prompt me not to drink but a half glass of milk. Whenever he suggested that, I knew I was going to get two bites of his ice cream. Mom would scowl but Dad argued that two small spoonfuls of vanilla ice cream were just about the same, in food value, as one-half glass of milk.

Dad was my pal.

3
Mom and Dad, Sports and Me

Add umph to try to get triumph.

Anonymous

When I was almost seven years old in the Summer of 1941, the diabetic specialist at Pittsburgh Children's Hospital called a family meeting. The appointment was to cover every aspect in the care of diabetes — what I could and could not do. What he said I could do was not much of a problem, but the things he put into the "Cannot Do" section were distressing. The list of Can't Do's made me feel as if I was being tied up by a rope. The list:

No gym class
No running
No roller skating
No bicycle riding
No baseball or other sports
No exercise of any kind.

In short, just sit around and basically, do nothing. How was a boy full of vim and vigor, supposed to just sit? At this meeting, I was told that if I should live to be 50 years of age, I would probably be blind.

In 1939, the widely held medical belief was that

exercise was bad because it burns sugar and, therefore, the sugar level could not be controlled. I suppose we all know that exercise burns sugar, but today, the physicians look on it much differently. Now, exercise is recommended routinely as part of the care of diabetics, and books are written on the subject.

Clearly, the medical profession was still learning the basic truths about diabetes. Still, I wonder how, with such confidence, this physician thought he could foretell the future. I was told I could not play baseball, but I played until I was 52. I quit touch tackle football at age 45. Because of a car accident, I was forced to give up basketball in 1998, playing my last game at age 62. As I get closer to the 70-year mark, I am presently on only my third eye glasses prescription. I need help when reading, as most folks past 50 do, but not for distance. When I umpire, I take off my eye glasses. Although I might have missed a call, it wasn't because I needed glasses!

However, the doctor sure "missed the call" on defining my life with diabetes. I believe I did not fulfill his prediction because I have taken good care of myself and have been darn lucky.

Each of us with Sugar Diabetes presents an individual case. We're not all alike, yet I believe we share the ability to do just about anything anyone else can do. Although I never went deep sea diving, I white water rafted. I never went sky diving, but I have ridden a few scary roller coasters. I never played soccer but I played baseball, football and basketball. Had soccer been more popular, I probably would have tried that sport also.

Type 1 diabetes has not kept Chris Dudley from a full and successful career as an NBA player. American Baseball League pitcher Dan Reichert continues to pitch for the Kansas City Royals. Olympians Gary Hall and Diane Muntz were not hindered by diabetes as they swam for gold medals in the 2000 games. Diabetes did not hamper the performance of baseball pro Ron Santo and many other professional and capable athletes. Not because they ignored it, but because they took care of themselves. We can say they took good care of their diabetes.

But I'm getting ahead of myself. When I was seven, Mom believed the doctor when he needlessly frightened her and said, "He can't."

Mom, Dad and Me

My happiness derives from knowing the people I love are happy. Emmanuel Kant

Mom was a picture of beauty, always dressing for the occasion, always with her hair of strawberry blond in place, and with hazel eyes that changed color when she wore her favorite shades of green.

Mom was born on a train, as it passed through a small town in Missouri. She never knew if the correct year was 1905 or 1906. Named Ollie after her mother's favorite sister, her tiny newborn body was kept warm by a handmade incubator, constructed out of heated bricks. Ollie's will to survive continued throughout her life. Education was important to her and she completed a business college degree she had once begun. In the typing class, she began at the bottom of the ranking and was not content until her name topped the list. Some years later on Easter Monday of 1930, in Cleveland, Ohio, she married W. Don Ray. My sister Geraldine "Gerri" was born two years later. Eventually, Mom changed "Ollie" to "Olive," a name she thought was much more sophisticated.

Mom not only gave me life in 1934, but she gave me life daily for years afterward. Each minute of each day she gave me nearly everything she had by tending to me in every way imaginable. She cooked and made sure I had the proper amounts of proper foods. She stopped baking cookies and cakes and began making pies, with a special sugar-free pie for me. She tested my sugar level and she made certain I had no cuts or injuries on my body, especially on my feet and legs, the areas most susceptible to infection. She complied with our family physician who told us NEVER to overlook even a slight nick or cut as poor circulation in the lower extremities of diabetics, coupled with infection can, in the worst cases, lead to hospital-ization and, too often, to gangrene and amputation. Diabetics must always take exceptional care of any cuts to their bodies.

In general, Mom spoiled me. But when it came to sports, or even exercise, Mom would never let me out of her sight. When I helped cut the grass, shovel snow or rake leaves, Mom seemed always to be in view, making sure that I didn't hurt myself or burn too much sugar and put myself into an insulin reaction.

With a baseball or a football, Dad and I would play catch in the backyard while Mom watched from a lawn chair. I don't know if she watched my father while we played, but I know she saw every move I made. Mom not only gave me her love, but she taught me what love is, that it is not only a feeling, but a concern for and a taking-care-of others.

In the spring and summer, Dad and I spent many evenings "playing" baseball. Late summer and fall were devoted to football.

Dad always loved a good game. There were stories from his youth that told of him and his friends breaking into a school late Saturday evening to borrow pads and helmets to play football on Sunday. They always returned the equipment before school began on Monday. A farm boy from the mid-west, Dad had been a big, strong kid for his age. As an adult, at 6 feet tall and weighing about 190 pounds, he was as handsome a man as Mom was pretty, even as his hairline receded. Although he didn't have much formal education, Dad's intelligence impressed me.

He was a master at crossword puzzles and had won contests. As a bridge player, he was the sought-after partner. Once, when I was having trouble with algebra, Dad offered to help. "Dad, this is algebra," I scoffed, "how are you going to help me with that?" His calm reply was, "Let's take a look and see if we can figure it out." He then proceeded by simple logic and arithmetic to generate the correct answer. We then went back through the text book to find the formal approach. Dad was the natural caretaker in charge of the weights and measures associated with my diabetes.

Dad was William Donald Ray, I was Donald William. I've always been proud of our close name association. We were both called Don, though I was Donny for a long time. Our initials comprise the raised artwork on Dad's gold ring.

Dad Understood

One of the greatest pleasures in life is doing something that someone said, "You can't." Anonymous

By the time I turned nine and we had moved back to Cleveland, Dad one evening asked me if I wanted to play on a baseball team. I almost jumped out of my skin with excitement. Yes, Yes, I wanted to play baseball! All my friends were playing and had been for the past several summers, but due to the doctor's instructions, I never played, other than with Dad. The neighborhood kids would invite me to play on their team, but I would always give them a "lame duck" excuse. Excuses like my mom needed me around the house to help with chores, or that Mom was concerned about my being hurt, that Mom wanted me to wait until I was older.

Finally, I would play! Dad never told anyone at Registration that I had sugar diabetes for fear they wouldn't let me sign-up. And, we didn't tell Mom that I was playing baseball. For years, it was Dad's and my secret. Because we were late in registering, I was assigned to a team that did not have any players from my immediate neighborhood. Perhaps that aided us in keeping the secret from Mom.

At every game I played, Dad was there. His job as sales manager of an auto-parts company gave him a flexible schedule. If we played twice a week, Dad would be there twice a week. His reason for attending was two-fold: he could watch his only son play ball, and he was constantly on the watch for my behavior, monitoring me closely for signs of low blood sugar.

To the games, Dad brought an Army canteen, half full of orange juice, fortified with sugar.

Occasionally I would need a drink of the "sugar juice" when a wing-ding would find its way into the game. I was blessed with pretty good speed and felt obligated to give my full effort to the team, never "short-cutting" my teammates by holding back because of diabetes. If I got a break from a bad hop or a misplayed ball, I was off for another base or two. I played the infield and pitched and so burned a lot of sugar. Dad was perceptive and would catch a wing-ding in the early stages. That Army canteen became a part of my baseball equipment that outlasted even my first ball glove.

For years, the only piece of equipment I owned was my treasured ball glove. The league supplied the shirts and caps. We all wore tennis shoes. I don't believe that I wore a pair of baseball shoes until I was a teenager. My father had his friend make a special bat for me on a lathe. I then had a homemade bat like comic strip character Ozark Ike. Ozark was a good ole Southern boy who could hit a baseball a mile. He was Babe Ruth, Ty Cobb and Honus Wagner all rolled into one. He would compare today to Alex Rodriguez, Manny Ramirez and Mark McGwire. The daily paper featured this comic strip favorite taking us on the escapades of this remarkable, fictitious ball player. My bat, like his, carried the carving "Ozark Ike." On the other side of my bat was carved "Don." I hit a "ton" with this bat, my prized possession. It was just the right size for a youngster and I used it until I was 12 years old.

At about the same time, Mom found out I had been playing ball.

Why sports?

To be a winner, you always come back, no matter what happened the day before. Billy Martin

In my childhood, two major things entered my life — sugar diabetes and sports. As to the diabetes, I had no choice, but why sports? I've been asked why sports have been important to me throughout my life. I explain my answer this way:

My love for sports began when, as a kid, Dad took me to Cleveland Indians ball games in the old League Park. At League Park Dad had watched Babe Ruth hit home runs. I was born a few years too late to see "The Babe," but I saw Ted Williams and Joe DiMaggio at the newer Cleveland Municipal Stadium that was built to house major league baseball. There I watched my favorite player, Lou Boudreau, #5.

At the same time, while I was learning to respect the game, I was told that I could never play it. I could not participate in ball games. Period. When I got the nod from Dad, and yes, finally from Mom, I wanted to be a part of what I was told I could not have. When I launched into my athletic life, I suppose it was to show the doctors that I could do it, but as time progressed, I began to totally enjoy the act of being a part of a team. Being a part of a group pulling together for the same end result. Yes, to win was the ultimate goal, but to do your best, even when losing, was acceptable if you gave it your best shot.

Telling me I couldn't participate may have been the motivator, but once I got there, once I learned that I could compete, there was no turning back. I learned the joy of a win, the joy of being part of something I could do. I made five my baseball number. I fell in love with the game and the striving to win.

I'm not alone, there are thousands upon tens of thousands of players that feel as I do. We even refer to it as having "heart" for the game. I spent many more hours in baseball competition but football was its equal in my love for sports. Basketball kept me in shape before baseball and after football.

Dad and I went to Cleveland Rams games before they moved to Los Angeles and then to St. Louis.

During my adolescence, The Cleveland Browns became a passion that has lasted a lifetime. With every day and year, "the game" became more desirable to me as I met more and more friends. As my skills improved and I became a bit better at the sport-of-the-season, I savored doing something special in my position, something that helped win a game. I enjoyed it when I received an award or accolades from my teammates. During the many, many times that I could have done something to win a game but failed to do so, I knew it was okay because "We have another game tomorrow. I will have another chance." I noticed the spark of excitement when I knew my parents, and later my wife and kids were proud of me for an accomplishment on the basketball court, the football "grid iron" or on the baseball field.

I learned my three sports as best I could. I learned to give all I had, never ask for favors, just do my best with the equipment God gave me. This, then, became my philosophy of life. On the playing field, my equipment consisted of bats, balls and teammates. In my adult life my "equipment" consists of houses, cars and families. I learned that equipment includes our health. It can be, and is for me, sugar diabetes. Sugar diabetes became part of my equipment, what I had to work with.

While my capabilities may not have been as plentiful as other's, I gave 100%. For every minute I spent on an athletic field, for every at bat, for every catch, for every tackle or yard gained, I am grateful. Sports have given me many pleasures and accomplishments — sports have been so very good to me. A life without sports and without diabetes would have been someone else's life, surely not mine.

Thanks to the doctor who said "You can't."

4

Coma
An important lesson learned

In the summer of 1948, with a new baby sister, Donna Lee, in the family, I believed that I could do anything anyone else could do. However, there was one thing I couldn't do: I could not eat candy or drink soda, or "pop," as we call it in Ohio. For that matter, anything not prescribed in my diet should not have been a part of my life.

At age 14, I discovered that the hard way.

We teens spent much time at the local playgrounds where we played baseball, several games daily. At some time during the day we would work in a game of marbles or "mumbly-peg." In the evening, when a few of us were allowed to stay out until the street lights came on, we played "kick the can," an outdoor game similar to hide and seek. Another favorite game was "capture the flag," a "war" game, played with teams attempting to capture the opponent's flag.

Marbles was a game where you had a shooting marble, usually your favorite, one of the many in your collection. There were two popular marble games – – one where we would draw a circle in the dirt, possibly a 6-foot circumference, and each player would scatter 3, 4 or 5 marbles within the circle. Each player would then attempt to knock an opponent's marble out of the circle with his shooting marble.

The shooter marble would be launched from the outer edge of the circle by balancing it on a partially curved index finger and then snapping it forward with a flick of the thumb. If the targeted marble was struck by the shooter, a second shot was then awarded and, almost certainly, the second shot would propel the enemy marble from the circle. This second shot was taken almost atop the competitor's marble. When a marble was knocked from the circle, it would then belong to the marksman.

Our second marble pastime was played over a larger field, possibly an area of 30 square feet. Holes were dug, approximately 6 inches around and 3 inches deep, spaced about 10 feet apart. The game was similar to croquet, with the holes acting as wickets and our shooting marble acting as the wooden ball. The object was to sink your marble into each hole around the course. The first to complete the course was declared the winner, and each of the losing companions would forfeit a marble to the winner. In both of these games, losing a marble was the player's penalty. We were proud of our bulging marble pouches.

Mumbly-peg was great fun but if one were to lose, he or she would have a very dirty face! The game was to place a fully-opened pocket knife, with the point down, first on your shoulder, then on your wrist, then on your forearm, then on your elbow. Your arm would be folded with your hand rested on your shoulder so that your elbow was the closest to the ground. You were to flip the knife from each of those positions and it was to land, sticking into the earth on which we knelt. Each competitor would progress from shoulder to elbow and back again from elbow to shoulder, four attempts going down and four attempts going back up for eight knife flips.

If the knife stuck into the ground you would get another turn from the next arm position. If the knife did not stick, your next attempt would begin at the failed position. The peg was a big part of the game, the peg being a sturdy 1/4 or 3/8 inch diameter twig from a nearby tree, sharpened at one end. When each player made a knife stick, he would use his knife handle to get one hit at the peg to drive it into the ground. The game was complete when there remained one participant that had not completed his/her eight flips. When this loser was declared, he or she was required to chew the peg out from the ground with his or her teeth! While doing this toothy digging, they were required to either talk or sing until the peg was shown to the winning players. Mumbly-peg, mumble while you dig for the peg! When we didn't get good hits on the peg, it wasn't too deep in the ground, but most of the time the peg was well out of sight. It was fun, even with those dirty faces.

At the recreational areas, morning and afternoon drinks and snacks were provided by the City of Cleveland. The playground attendants, often school teachers with summer jobs and aware of my diabetes, had sweetened juice ready for me. Mom made certain of that.

After our day at the park, the guys and gals ordered drinks, like a red pop, at the local fountain. You never heard anyone order cherry – it was always red pop. Another favorite was a chocolate phosphate. It was made with a generous amount of chocolate syrup mixed with soda water. Few drinks then were purchased bottled, canned or in a carton. Usually they were created at the fountain of a drug store, diner or restaurant using what we called "fizz water." Sometimes I would order a small carton of milk although I usually drank water because the refreshments offered at the park were enough and were based on my diet.

Who Was I Fooling?

One summer day, I had my first chocolate phosphate. I felt I was in good shape and took care of myself, and so, what the heck, I can do that. You can't imagine how good that tasted. I was 14 years old and had not tasted anything like that in my entire life. IT WAS GOOD. IT WAS REALLY GOOD! After that went down, I felt fine and I tried another one — it tasted better than the first. I can't recall exactly, but I might have consumed three in that one sitting. When I went home to test my urine for my sugar count, it was a 4+, meaning over 400, and slightly red, mostly brown in color, indicating that my system was loaded with sugar.

I fibbed to my mother and told her I had a 1+, just a little sugar in my system. I also cheated in marking the chart we kept. I continued to take my normal dosage of insulin and eat my normal, weighed dinner. I became very, very tired. I went to bed but as I remember, went to the toilet many times during the night. The next morning I took a bigger dose of Regular (fast-acting) as well as Protamine (long-lasting) insulin, with the hope that I could counteract my high sugar level. Of course, I did not tell Mom about these added units. I just kept cheating.

For the next several days, I followed the same routine — play ball all day, go to the deli with my friends, drink another phosphate or orange pop, go home at 5:00 dinner time, check my sugar level, notice it was sky high again, lie to Mom and then sit down to eat dinner as if nothing was wrong. As one day passed into another, it just became worse and worse. As I continued on the same ignorant path, it seemed the more sugared sodas I drank, the more I had to have.

Soon my saliva became as thick as paste. My visits to the lavatory became so frequent that it was a subject of conversation with my friends. "What, again?" they questioned. My obsession for something to drink was almost embarrassing. My thirst was never satisfied. When I took a drink, it normalized the pasty, white cotton saliva, but quickly the thickness would return. When drinking water from a faucet or fountain, it provided some relief to the tormenting saliva, but when I had the chance to consume an ice cold soda pop or phosphate, it seemed to relieve me a little more and for a little longer. Besides, those drinks tasted so much better than water.

This went on for about a week. Each day my urine test results would seem to be a more ugly reddish-brown, and I continued to lie to my parents. If Mom would ask to see the test results, I would pour out some of the true color and add Benedict Solution, the bluish liquid that I used to test my urine, until the color was an acceptable aqua or light green.

Altering the insulin dosage, I would take a unit more, then two units more, then three. I cannot honestly tell how many extra units I took each day. Near the end of that week, I was taking extra insulin in the morning, sneaking a shot into my system when I first returned home, and then taking extra along with the normal dinner-hour injection. Without these added injections, I might have gone into a coma then, but all I was doing was prolonging the inevitable.

Excessive thirst was never so prevalent. I just could not get enough to drink and I could hardly go 30 minutes without a trip to the lavatory. This was, by far, worse than when it was first discovered that I had sugar diabetes. Much worse!

Not only were my thirst and urination affected, but my stamina weakened such that I could play only one baseball game, not the anticipated two or three. My skills began to deteriorate. My "go-go" was gone and I became listless. The guys even had me hitting down in the batting order, not in my usual prestigious 3rd or 4th spot. Who did I think I was fooling? I wasn't fooling them.

Big Trouble

I do not know the exact date, but for certain it was August. Early in the morning, at 2:00 or 3:00 a.m., I knew I was in trouble. Big time trouble. I had broken into a cold sweat, I was freezing, I was trembling, my saliva was too thick to describe. I felt I could urinate continually. I felt as if I was going to die. I am not sure how nearing death may feel, but I think that it must be just as it was then. The journey down the hallway to my parents' room seemed to be an endless tunnel toward my own demise. I did not think I would make it, but I reached my parents' bedside and awakened my father.

"Dad, I need help," I slurred. Instantly he knew that it was an emergency as that may have been the first time I ever asked anyone for physical help. He could not see me in the dark, but he knew. Mom also woke. When the light was turned on and their eyes fixed on me, it was even more evident that I was in serious trouble. Mom later described how I looked: I was foaming at the mouth; I was the color of a white sheet with eyes that appeared to be glass; my shirt was wringing wet and my skin was slippery wet. I wasn't fooling them anymore either.

We got into Dad's car and drove to the nearest hospital. The last thing I remember before falling into unconsciousness was the bright red neon sign over the entrance driveway that read, "Emergency." Passing out was similar to quietly and slowly falling asleep. I drifted into a deep coma, one that would last for a week and a half. Eleven days of my life that I cannot account for.

When I entered Lutheran Hospital, my weight was about 140 pounds. When I was released more than two weeks later, my weight was under 100 pounds. For eleven days I had no solid food, just intravenous feedings of insulin and nourishment. My blood sugar level at the onset of the coma was 785. With a number that high, death was lurking around the corner. The medical professionals at the hospital tried desperately to get my sugar count out of the danger zone while simultaneously giving me enough intravenous calories to sustain life. They knew that I was in this condition because I had "overdosed" on sugar, and "abused" my body. My friends were available to fill in details of my visits to the soda fountain.

Fifty years ago, there were countless different theories on treating diabetes. The staff physicians on my case each had their own views on my situation and disagreed on how it should be managed. Diabetic specialists were consulted and they, too, had differing opinions. Some felt that too much insulin, in large doses, would be too hard on my extremely weakened condition. They wanted to limit the dosage, keeping it controlled with slow, gradual intravenous drips.

This was the avenue they chose to follow. My sugar count remained in the high 700s. Gradually, and unbeknown to me, my life was slipping away.

Doctor Roenigk's Decision

After a few days, our family physician, Doctor Henry H. Roenigk, Sr., was called in for his opinion. Doctor Roenigk was a straight shooter who always told it as it was. No colorful language, no cushioning, no beating around the bush, just his gravel voice and the confidence that he knew his patients. Up to that point, we had every good faith in his medical knowledge and Mom and Dad certainly had no reason to question him now. The general feeling by the present medical staff was that the chances of my pulling through were very slim. They continued to think that if large insulin doses were given, it would prove fatal. Doctor Roenigk consulted with my family and took charge of my case. He ordered insulin injections to begin and to continue with a steady intravenous flow throughout the day and night. Plus, additional injections of Regular insulin were to be administered every four hours. The intravenous insulin feedings were now not only in both arms, but in both thighs and my stomach.

Huge quantities of insulin were now being pumped into my system. In response to the argument that large doses would kill me, Doctor Roenigk responded, "He is dying anyway. What is there to lose?" He was right on both counts, and the added insulin saved my life.

The Value of Life

I had the good fortune to pull away from near-death. I realized then that the coma was a wake-up call for me. When I opened my eyes from the coma, I also "opened my eyes" to how precious life is. I realized, too, the suffering I caused my family. Had I fallen through death's door, those remaining, Mom, Dad and Gerri, as well as friends and other relatives, would continue to feel pain. The old comment, "death is most difficult for the living," became real to me at this young age. I realized, too, that my dumb, careless attitude almost eliminated the special things that were to become my life. Like Jimmy Stewart's character in *It's A Wonderful Life*, I would have missed out on many wonderful things.

The things I did, good or bad in the 50 years since my coma would never have happened. It would have been unforgivable to miss so much. I would never have experienced the touch of my wife's hand, never helped to create my four children and our nine grandchildren, and relish in their accomplishments. I would have never gotten to know my then tiny baby sister. I would never have gotten a passing grade in Algebra and a failing grade in German. I would never have met people that became my friends. I would never have gotten that key base hit that won a game, never a tackle that saved a game, never a dropped fly ball that cost us a tournament. Never experienced the big and small things that are life.

Diabetes was given to me for a reason: because God felt I could handle it. The coma was generated solely because I was diabetic, but, ironically, it gave me a taste of life's sweetness, life's sugar, by allowing me to stay here for awhile longer — to stay and to totally appreciate all that has been placed before me. I can give thanks to my condition for letting me know the value of life, and the value of what one can accomplish while here.

I repeat, diabetes really never changed my life — it is basically all I ever knew, but it helped me to lead a better life.

The Lady in the White Dress

Some people make the world special just by being in it.

Anonymous

Eleven days later I regained consciousness. I recall vividly looking about the room and questioning, "Where am I?" I had no idea what day it was or who that woman was sitting by my bedside in a white dress. Everything was a total mystery to me.

I could not identify the lady in the white dress, but it seemed that somehow I did know her. Maybe I had met her somewhere, maybe she was an aunt of a neighbor, or the mother of a friend I saw at school. When I first looked at her, she was asleep. When my movements startled her awake, she smiled ever so sweetly as she looked into my eyes and said, "Hello, Donald, it's good to see you." I can remember that comment and see her face as if this just happened yesterday. This was one of those moments that you never forget.

As it turned out, Eileen was a nurse's aide. Her

duties at the hospital were in the ward to which I was assigned, and during her scheduled shift and on her own time, she would make routine visits to my room. Eileen had lost her son in an automobile accident, and she still grieved the loss. Her son and I apparently resembled each other and were close in age. When she could, she would spend her time sitting by my side and, in her loving, caring way, did everything she could for me. I understand she would arrive early for her work shift to spend additional time with me.

I was later told that during my "blackout" period, I would occasionally regain consciousness for a moment or two. I realized it was then that I would see Eileen's face before me. There is no telling how frequently these awakenings happened, but evidently they were often enough. The vision of her was so imbedded in my mind that when I awoke, I thought I already knew her.

So, in fact, I had seen her. She had been, along with my parents, my companion during that dark journey. The vision of her from the twilight space of my coma stayed with me strongly and prominently. Eileen befriended my parents by offering them encouragement, and by assuring them that the best care was being given to me. Eileen did more than her share to make me well. She was one special lady. We kept in touch via telephone for a couple of years, but eventually lost contact with one another . . .

. . . until, in 1986, almost 40 years later, we received a call from a woman, asking if this was the residence of Donald Ray that had Sugar Diabetes. That particular day was my son's tenth birthday and I remember it quite well. My son Scott had answered, gave me the phone and said that someone was calling about sugar diabetes. She introduced herself to me as Eileen, and advised that she had been out of town for several years, had now been stricken with cancer, but wanted to know if I was okay and doing well. Hearing her voice was a delightful surprise! I attempted to arrange a meeting, a luncheon, just a simple get-together, but she declined each of my suggestions. I told her I would certainly like to see her, I hoped she could meet my family, but she would not give me an affirmative response. She said she was living with her sister and gave me that telephone number.

I called about a week later to attempt a meeting. Eileen's sister answered and explained that Eileen had passed away a few days earlier. This sad news almost took my breath away. My knees grew weak. Her sister went on to say that Eileen had often spoken about the diabetic boy in the hospital who reminded her of her son. She knew she was on her deathbed, but wanted to leave this earth knowing that the boy she cared for was well.

Eileen, enjoy your stay in Heaven. I hope that someone is tending to you, just as you did for me. When my turn comes, I am going to look you up and I won't let you say no to me again. Maybe then we can have that lunch.

God bless you.

5
Return to Life

I never felt that I didn't have a chance to win.

Arnold Palmer

My Vow — After the coma, I made a vow. I vowed to myself that when I pass on, when the good Lord decides to take me, MY DEATH WILL NOT BE DUE TO SUGAR DIABETES. I may have a heart attack, I may get struck by a car, but I will not "cash in my chips" due to the fact that I have diabetes.

I will do this by following these diabetic rules.

Don's Diabetic's Rules

1 I will continue to eat wisely and monitor what I eat.
2 I will continue to take my insulin and meals at approximately the same time each day.
3 I will test my sugar level at least three times daily, every day, and definitely before going to bed at night.
4 I will continue to avoid sweets and alcoholic beverages.
5 I will have routine medical and eye examinations.
6 I will continue to exercise and will, in short, follow

the diabetic rules.

7　I will be mindful that I do not fool anyone by
sneaking something I should not be eating or
drinking.

These rules are not that difficult. In short, they
require that I work with my physician to establish a
plan to manage my diabetes and then follow the plan.

*Through rigorous scientific studies, scientists are
now certain that tightly controlled blood glucose
levels can delay the development of diabetic
complications in most people.*"
(from "Countdown" — a publication by the Juvenile
Diabetes Research Foundation, Summer, 2000)

With no disrespect intended, science is now
certain about many things I have always known or
believed because I have lived with diabetes on a daily
and hourly basis for more than six decades. I know
to check my blood sugar before going to bed at night
because that is the time a body goes into a fast. For
about six to nine hours during the night, we receive
no nutrition. Although the NPH insulin helps keep
my sugar at moderate levels while I sleep, a low blood
sugar, a hypoglycemic reaction, can result. In my
experiences, I have found it is very difficult for family
members to bring me out of a wing-ding when they
discover it in the middle of the night. To administer
juice or packaged glucose to me is often a hardship
on those trying to help. I try to have my sugar level
at a count of 150 to 170 before going to bed. In the
morning, my sugar level is usually consistent at 110
to 125, thanks in part to the NPH. Diabetics need
to be in touch with their physicians about this and

other times that low sugar levels (or high levels) are likely to occur. It was morning hypoglycemic reactions that resulted in officers Kelly and Jim being called to help me.

When my diet was arranged, Doctor Roenigk asked what I preferred to eat at each meal and then prescribed the amount of insulin to that amount of food. So frequently my insulin was prescribed to meet what other physicians decided I should eat. I refer to my doctor's approach as an Insulin to Food Plan, while the other system is a Food to Insulin Plan. I remember many days when I had been constantly hungry; I wasn't getting enough calories to sustain my active lifestyle. When I confronted Doctor Roenigk with that, he calmly took out a pad and pencil and asked, "What would you like to eat?" As the consumption of food varies, so does the insulin, and his nurse then calculated the amount of insulin needed based on the calorie count. Often the success of the diet was trial and error, but usually he was right on target. For years, when my schedule was very active, I stuck with the 6,000 calories daily program, matched to the correct amount of insulin.

When recovering from the coma, after not having eaten any solid food for ten days, I was given vanilla wafer cookies and jello. I became attached to those wafers and jello and I asked Doctor Roenigk if he would be able to work them into my diet. He and his staff figured out that I could offset my morning and afternoon snacks with vanilla wafers in place of the crackers or chips. I still enjoy vanilla wafers and jello, but I don't enjoy them to the point that they, or any food or drink, will be harmful to my sugar/insulin balance.

A "Little Extra" Insulin

As I think back on the diabetic coma, I took a "little extra" insulin to combat my high sugar count. Not good! In my tenure with diabetes, the number of times that I have "legitimately" needed to take an "added" dose of insulin can be counted on one hand. I strongly feel that a diabetic just cannot regulate or control his or her life by eating whatever is desired, and then attempt, notice this word, attempt, to correct everything by another dose or two or more of insulin. It did not work before my coma and I do not believe it is the way to manage diabetes. Time and research will tell us if this holds true even for those on "the pump," a relatively new device worn on the body that releases insulin into the system on an as-needed basis. I believe that WE, not a device or a machine, need to manage our diabetes.

The pump, like the syringe, is not a cure, but a tool to help us. If diabetics rely solely on our tools, without understanding the hows and whys of their condition, without learning to respect the condition, how will they ever learn to manage it should something happen to the pump or to the syringe? If we don't understand diabetes, how will we help ourselves if other indicators should get out of balance even if the tools are functioning properly? It holds true, as well, for Type 2 diabetics (those whose bodies produce some insulin but require supplements) who take tablets to stimulate insulin production, that knowledge of and respect for diabetes are extremely important. I cannot believe that whether we take insulin by the pump, a syringe or a tablet, that diabetics can merrily eat anything desired and hope to make up for it with doses of insulin without having some consequences to pay. We do not want these consequences to be "complications," the name used to cover blindness and loss of limbs, not to mention the high blood pressure that can result from obesity.

Instead of worrying about *indulgence, convenience* and what I am or am not *deprived* of, I concentrate on concepts of KNOWLEDGE, MODERATION, DISCIPLINE, REGIMENTATION, CONSIST-ENCY and RESPECT. These are the ideas I use when approaching the care of diabetes: Knowledge is needed in understanding diabetes and the important role the balloon-like organ, the pancreas, has in producing insulin. Respect is due the insulin, the hypodermic needles, syringes, the health care professionals and researchers that make control possible. Moderation is needed in approaching sugar "treats," even, I believe, when using the insulin pump. A disciplined life reaps rewards in not only caring for diabetes but in caring for areas of our professional and personal lives, as well. These ideals have carried over into my life in sports, and have been reinforced because of sports. A diabetic, to be "successful," must understand the disorder and establish a plan that works, a regime, and follow it consistently. These are attitudes and actions that we are neither too old nor too young to learn. These are the thoughts and actions that have worked for me.

Back to School

After recuperating from the coma, I began junior high school. While I was in school and for several years afterward, what stood out in my mind about that coma summer, which my own stupidity

53

and bad choices caused, was that I missed four weeks of the new semester, particularly my language class, German. When I entered the class for the first time, I was completely lost as students were speaking German almost exclusively. It was truly a foreign world and I could not catch up fast enough. I failed German and had to retake the class. The second time through I was well ahead of my incoming classmates, but I lost an entire year. When in my junior year I could have scheduled another class, such as literature, speech or even wood shop, I needed that hour for my second year of German. I lost five hours of each school week that deprived me of taking another subject and learning something new.

My new classmates found out soon enough about my diabetes. If they hadn't heard about the coma, they learned of my condition during this first year because of a low sugar reaction in my English class, just before lunch. The school offered two lunch periods and I was scheduled for the later one. After this episode, my lunch was moved forward: I felt a wing-ding coming on just minutes before class ended. I thought I might not be too far into this reaction and could get to the cafeteria. I took a sugar cube that I had in my pocket, but it wasn't enough. I put my head down on my desk, on top of the essay I had written for class. As I began to perspire, the ink (we had no ball point pens) on the paper became a splotch of blue coloring on my face. I dozed off into a sound sleep.

The teacher called for the school nurse — both were aware of my condition — and they were able to get some sugar into my system. With the help of some schoolmates, they placed me in a wheel chair and took me to the second-floor elevator. When we arrived downstairs, I was wheeled through the entire cafeteria to reach the juices and food I needed. One lunch period was just ending, the second was just beginning, and countless students saw the sight of this blue-faced boy. The next several days found me explaining why my face was blue and why I was in a wheel chair. Their reaction to my diabetes was one of curiosity and interest.

Play Ball

It's very, very difficult to beat a person that never gives up. Babe Ruth

At age 14, I was playing basketball for the school and I was the shortest player on the team, but because I was fast, I played point guard. When I reached the ninth grade, however, my entire school sports career took a severe tumble. The school physician informed my family that I could not participate in any school sport. Apparently my lengthy hospital stay and coma prompted the doctor to make the decision. I was devastated. I had suspected that because of the coma my fall and winter sports would be jeopardized, but I felt I could at least play baseball that coming spring. For gosh sakes, I just made the basketball team and now I had to turn in my uniform! Further, I had already played with many of the varsity baseball players the previous summer. I really wanted to play ball. This, not the diagnosis of diabetes, was my first experience in learning that life could be so unfair.

Meanwhile, all year I participated in athletics outside the school. My baseball skills, so I was told, were good enough that at age 13 I was invited to play on a team of older fellows (16 years and under)

from the surrounding neighborhoods. The competition here was much tougher. I was nicknamed "Little Ray" not only because I was young but because I was small for my age. At the beginning, I was almost overwhelmed with the size and talent of many of the older kids. Although I had played infield and pitched before, my pitching wasn't strong enough at this level, and so I moved to shortstop and played for this coach during the next three seasons. I still had many fundamentals to learn but our coach was a fine teacher. Many of his thoughts and ideas influenced me when I began coaching.

After waiting a semester, Dad tried everything he could to convince the school officials that it was all right for me to play. A letter from Doctor Roenigk did not help, a letter from our congressman did not help, nor did a letter from my father advising that the family would accept full responsibility for any injuries. This fell on deaf ears.

I continued to play football on a City team, and baseball in the neighborhood and in summer leagues. When I reached 16, I moved to a baseball league designed for 18- and 19-year olds. I was targeted by the older guys (some were college players) as my smaller size and known age were an apparent insult to them. Coach felt their attitudes were, to quote, "warped." Nearly half the season passed before I could prove to them that my skills were good enough to earn me the right to play in their league, and I was at last accepted.

Eventually, a new physician was assigned to the school. Thankfully, his approach was much different from his predecessor's and the restriction on me was lifted. I was finally able, in my senior year, to play a high school sport. I played varsity baseball and received my only varsity letter. All of my teammates, the same guys that played in the summer leagues with me, were gracious enough to elect me captain. I was honored by this gesture.

After graduation in the fall of 1952, I played amateur football in the City league. Because my mother insisted, I wore a helmet with a built-in face mask to protect my teeth. This big plastic mask was hideous and rendered me unrecognizable. The football coach from my former high school happened to be watching us play one afternoon. I was having a satisfying day quarterbacking. "Who is that at quarterback?" he asked. I heard him. He came over as I took of my helmet. "Ray?" He was stunned. "I didn't know you could play like that." My reply, "I tried to tell you for four years, Coach!"

The Globetrotters

Anger is only one letter short of danger. Anonymous

The Harlem Globetrotters, a popular and entertaining professional basketball team, then and now, toured the country. They are clever in their approach to the game and display "trick" plays to the delight of the crowd. Balls would spin like a top on their fingertips and then seem to disappear under legs and over shoulders. The opposition, of course, was a part of the act. It was both humorous and skillful at the same time.

For my sixteenth birthday, Dad got us seats for an upcoming game that featured the Globetrotters. I was ecstatic. The game was about two months away, but the anticipation of that date was such a thrill.

Looking forward to it might have been as exciting as the game. Not quite but almost. Game day arrived and it seemed as if Dad would never get home from work and we'd never get going.

He had planned to have dinner at a sports theme restaurant, and to leave the white scale behind. The game was at 8:00 PM at the old Cleveland Arena, and dinner reservations were at 6:00. Dad got home from work with a "loaner" automobile as his car was being repaired. We started to the dinner and game and I was about to burst with excitement. As always, I brought my insulin and would take the injection just before eating. We arrived in plenty of time and Dad found a parking spot near the front of the restaurant. As was now our going-out-to-dinner scenario, I took my shot in the car on this comfortable September night. We put the insulin bottle inside a thermos containing crushed ice, and the syringe, cotton, etc., into their container, and deposited all in the dashboard glove box. We entered the restaurant.

Dad, the great storyteller, kept me entertained during our meal. When dinner was finished, I was getting nervous as I knew we had farther to go to reach the arena, but Dad felt we had plenty of time. If Dad felt that way, it was good enough for me. We went out to the car and as Dad opened my door, we were immediately attacked by what seemed to be an army of men.

They forced both of us against the car, kicked our feet apart and pressed us tight against the side of the car. Dad was never one to be pushed around, even by these policemen, and it required three officers to hold him, while only one had me in check.

As they handcuffed him, he stated with conviction, "Don't hurt my boy, don't hurt my boy. If you hurt him you'll all pay for it." After Dad blared these statements, it felt as if they loosened their grip on me.

Because the officers would not tell my father what the problem was, he was as irate as I had ever seen him. I was pleased that they had restraints on his wrists behind his back. We were searched and our pocket contents placed on the car hood. One officer explained that he was going to open the car. He said that they had received a telephone call from a bus passenger that had noticed two men in a tan car, near the Elmira Restaurant, who were taking drugs. When the police arrived, they checked the license plate on the loaner and found that the plates had been reported stolen by the car dealer. It looked suspicious to the police officers. I guess it would: two drug addicts in a stolen car. That sounded serious to me.

When this information finally came out, Dad was allowed to reply. Prior to this, any comment was cut off with a "Shut up!" from the officers. Dad told them to open the glove box, open the thermos and look at the vial of insulin, clearly marked. The syringe was glass and rested in its sterling metal container. The insulin bottle was loose in the thermos. At the same time, one of the officers called the auto agency, the dealer that had reported the stolen plates, and was informed that those exact plates were no longer missing, but the agency had failed to notify the police department. The agency also told the officer that the car had been loaned to Mr. W. Don Ray. From wallet identification cards, the officers already knew my father's name.

The police were extremely apologetic and Dad had a few unpleasant words for them. He complained that we would now be late for the opening tip-off of the Harlem Globetrotter game. Now, it was twenty minutes to game time. The officers said, "Follow us." They proceeded to give us a police escort to the arena, allowed us to park in a special reserved spot, and then had our tickets exchanged for front-row passes. We practically sat on the floor of the basketball court. The officers redeemed themselves in our eyes. Almost.

The evening had a little of every emotion — fun, fear, anger, frustration and delight. It was one more occasion where we were reminded that the insulin shots that we took in stride were actually a noteworthy event. What appeared as strange and unusual behavior to everyone else was routine for us. The syringe that was life-saving to me seemed life-threatening to others, as was the case with the bus rider who jumped to conclusions. It is also true of my diabetic life that on several occasions people thought that my symptoms of a wing-ding were signs that I was drunk from excessive alcohol intake. There were times that someone would laugh or point a finger at this guy, me, that was stumbling. They failed to consider other possibilities. I suppose all of us will jump to wrong conclusions from time to time, yet it's good to remember that everything may not be as it seems at a glance.

This was a memorable night to share with my father.

Korean War

Even if you have pains, try not to be one. <small>Anonymous</small>

I graduated from John Marshall High in 1952 and, uncertain about my career objectives and whether I wanted to go to college, I began a job at Cleveland Welding. For the next year and a half, I helped to manufacture Roadmaster bicycles.

My Draft Board Physical

At that time, the Korean "war," officially called a "police action," was at full scale. Many of my classmates joined one of the armed services, or were drafted. At age 18, it was necessary for all young men to register with the Draft Board and then, when called, take a physical examination at a government facility. When I received my notification and reported, there were several hundred others reporting dutifully, as well.

I recall my feelings as we were lined up along the wall in single file. There was no alphabetical name system, just "Get at the end of the line." I thought about war. I had seen documentaries and Hollywood films of World War II that had ended just six years earlier. My high school had already lost young men to the Korean War effort. I later learned that three of our 1952 graduates lost their lives in Korea.

The exam was fairly routine. They checked our eye and hand coordination, vision, weight, took blood samples, checked for hernias and had each of us do a series of calisthenics, and then checked our hearts and lungs. When the testing was completed, we were sent home with the knowledge that a draft card containing our physical ranking, would be sent to our mailing address. The rankings appeared as a series of numerical symbols and alpha letters. Each number and letter meant something. Two rankings, 1A and 4F, every household in America knew — 1A indicated you were perfectly healthy and had no disabilities or problems that would keep you from military service. A ranking 4F meant you were not physically fit for military duty. Diabetes ensured a 4F rating, or so I thought.

When I entered the large gymnasium of the Old Armory building used for these kinds of activities, I explained to an attendant in a white coat that I was diabetic. His reply was, "Get back in line." I attempted to mention this again to another white-coated person, but his response was the same. "Get back in line" was a favorite phrase, and not just to me. We all went through the various stages of the physical. On four occasions I attempted to talk to someone. It crossed my mind that I should not have had my sugar so well controlled, and I thought: wouldn't it be ironic if they rated me 1A.

We were instructed not to talk unless spoken to by one of the uniformed personnel. I managed to sneak in a few words to the recruits to my left and right. I'm sure most were frightened but it was not visible. Their thoughts were varied with some wanting to go and others completely the opposite. No one, however, said, "I won't go." In 1952 our attitude was, "I'll go if I must." Period.

Within a week I received my draft card. I was classified as 1A, physically fit. Yes, I was fit in so many ways. To look at me or at any young diabetic, or to check our hearts, lungs, eyes and even urine if our sugar level is under control, one wouldn't find evidence that we are unable to serve in active military service during wartime. We could certainly fill most of the requirements and many of the duties, but it might be a bit difficult on a battlefield to ask the enemy to take a time-out while we visit the refrigerator to get our insulin!

My parents were distressed, especially Mom. Our first phone call was to the local army station. We were given the red-tape runaround before finding the proper person who instructed me to return for another physical with a written letter from our doctor, as well as one from our councilman.

The following week, Dad accompanied me. Before reporting, we stopped at an ice cream parlor and ordered a chocolate sundae to be sure my blood test would reveal high sugar. To indulge in ice cream was a rare occurrence for me and chocolate syrup was the impossible dream! As we entered the Old Armory, I saw many of the same white-gowned attendants. Dad sat while I again stripped down to my underwear and began to go through the same check points: eye-hand, vision, weight. My letters were handed to a uniformed military man and I re-dressed to join my father. After about an hour, another military man approached and cordially invited us into a nearby office. There we were greeted by a uniformed man who introduced himself as a physician.

The doctor asked that we sit down and the comedy of errors continued. He then "informed" us that my blood sugar level was extremely high, which was, of course, no surprise to us. He expressed his thanks that my father was in attendance, and then continued to advise that there was a very strong possibility that I might have Sugar Diabetes. I

MIGHT have diabetes! I thought my father was going to hit the ceiling! Why in the world did they think we had an appointment? Why had we given them the two required letters that now rested in plain view on the doctor's desk? The doctor was asked all of these questions and more, with passion. We were amazed that they were so inattentive and negligent. Finally, I was ranked 4F and could not serve in the Korean War effort.

My experience was not as rare as one would suppose. Because so many diabetics look, and are, healthy in many ways, physicians, school nurses and others often misdiagnose or overlook the condition. I heard about a child who was prescribed antibiotics instead of being treated for her Type 1 diabetes.

In the next chapter, an incident I refer to as "The King of all Wing-Dings" tells of a doctor who did all the right things. As you read the conclusion to that event, imagine what might have happened to me if the doctor had not immediately asked the important question, "Are you a diabetic?" Imagine if he had assumed that I was having an epileptic seizure or suffered from a degenerative muscular disease. Diabetes may not be visible, but it is our constant, internal companion.

6
On My Own

Adversity is a fact of life. It cannot be controlled.
What we can control is how we react to it.

Anonymous

Ohio University

Eventually, in January of 1954, I enrolled at Ohio University located in Athens, a few hours from our home. Because many of my high school friends, now sophomores, were members, I pledged *Phi Kappa Tau* fraternity as "frat" life offered a variety of extra opportunities to create close friendships, for intramural sports and the familiar fraternity parties. I enjoyed those "drunken fraternity parties" though I did not drink.

I've tasted one beer in my lifetime, one beer, just to know the taste, which I didn't like. I never did drink, and on most occasions I know I had more fun than those who did.

College life was my first experience being away from home and it took awhile getting used to it. Mom had always been there to guide my diabetes, but now, I was on my own. My biggest initial problem was the quantity of food that was served. It wasn't nearly enough to balance my insulin intake. I tried to adjust the insulin dosage to meet the minimal food I was receiving, but it just didn't work out well, and I experienced an insulin reaction a couple of times a week. The meals consisted of milk, dry cereal or toast and orange juice for breakfast — a sandwich, a drink of some sort, and once in a while soup and usually jello for lunch. Dinner might be closer to what is thought of as the "big" meal of the day, but it also fell short. My prescribed diet was still 6,000 calories a day; I was getting half that amount.

As a result, wing-dings were becoming too common and I had a meeting with the dietitian to see if an adjustment could be made. She was quite receptive to this and my parents had Doctor Roenigk mail a suggested diet plan to her. From that point on, I ate just as I would have at home. The ladies working in the cafeteria were marvelous. Often one of them would come out from the kitchen to check that I had all the calories I needed, and if the selections were satisfactory. They took special care to "spoil me," as if I was now their adopted son.

The second week of school my speech class was assigned in a building unfamiliar to me. I consulted a campus map and thought I could get specific directions on the first day of the class. When I awoke that morning, a low blood sugar reaction was starting to set in. I knew it was coming on but felt I would have enough time to dress, grab some food with extra orange juice, and get to class on time. I put on my jacket and headed to the cafeteria, passing the usual breakfast line of students as my control was beginning to leave me. I could not chance losing my balance and falling so I went directly to the orange juice tray. I tried to get granulated sugar into a glass of juice, but could not as my coordination was now starting to fail. One of the female students saw that I was having trouble and gave me assistance getting sugar into the glass. In the meantime, I gulped down a glass of juice. The second glass of juice, with the sugar, got me to a stable condition and I was back to normal. They offered toast that morning, and, taking a few pieces, I ate them on the way as I headed for class.

After asking for directions, I found the classroom but I was about ten minutes late. All the seats were occupied except the front, center desk. I had no choice but to sit myself right there in the front of the room. The professor made a terse comment: "Class starts at 8:00; let's not make a habit of this," and he asked my name. When the professor was to the side of the room, I felt it was a good moment to remove my jacket and not create another disturbance. I stood, removed my jacket and much to my embarrassment realized that I had forgotten, in the morning rush, to put on a shirt. My bare torso generated laughter from my fellow students and another terse remark from the professor: "It is customary to wear clothes in my classroom, please do so." That was one of those mornings you wish you could forget, and one more reminder of living with the consequences of diabetes.

Once my food intake was regulated, insulin reactions came under control. However, I experienced one wing-ding that remains in my memory because it added a touch of humor to an otherwise alarming event.

At a fraternity softball game against our arch rival *Sigma Nu*, I took my position at short stop. We were the home team and therefore batted in the last half of the inning. When we retired their last batter of the inning, I was the first batter for our team. Just as I stepped into the batter's box, a hypoglycemic reaction began to set in and my vision began to have double images. The first pitch was called a strike. I stepped out and asked for time. Our coach came from the bench and I told him I was starting to have a wing-ding. All my teammates, as well as each of my fraternity brothers knew of my diabetes, and a bag of gum drop candies was kept in the medical container at both of my "homes" for this situation – – my homes being my fraternity house and our bench at a ball diamond. My dorm room had its sugar cache, as well.

The umpire wanted to get the game moving and ordered me back to home plate. The coach opened our medical box and found just one piece of candy on hand. It was determined that some of my teammates had shared in this bounty that was apparently too handy in our first-aid kit. We only had nine players so that removing me from the game was not a thought. In baseball, once you are removed from the game, you cannot re-enter. Coach handed me the one little piece and told me to get in there and hit. I replied that there were two balls coming at me. He called back, as he started to run to the nearest store: "Just swing in the middle and you'll hit one of them."

I did. I swung right in the exact middle of the "two" balls and hit a dribbler of a ground ball back to the pitcher, and he threw me out at first base. Fortunately I did not lose muscle control of my legs and got back to the bench without incident. A few of the guys came out to lend assistance though none was necessary. The next few hitters stalled as best they could to give our coach enough time to return.

There would have been no way I could have played shortstop or even kept my balance without a sugar pick-me-up. The coach returned before long with the candy and also an orange drink.

Very quickly I was back to normal and, as memory serves me, I had a fairly good game, no-errors, a couple of hits, a couple of runs scored and we won the game. Not bad for a guy that had a wing-ding. When diabetics recover, we tend to recover quickly with no telltale signs that there had been an incident. Being prepared for a reaction to occur was critical on a ball field, however.

In the fall of 1955, I transferred my credits to Baldwin Wallace, a private college closer to home in Berea, Ohio, from which Gerri had graduated. At the time of my transfer, I could not anticipate how fortunate this move would prove to be. Dad was ailing, and I was soon to be needed at home.

The Loss of Dad

Good friends are like stars in heaven. You may not always see them, but they are always there. Anonymous

While attending Baldwin Wallace, I lived with my family in a brick bungalow on 149th Street of Cleveland's west side. My sister Gerri was now married with a little son, Jimmy, and Donna, at seven, was earning her title as kid sister when Dad became ill. We never imagined that the leg pain he experienced was other than a bump, a bruise or a muscle pull. Dad never complained but every now and then he would say, "Sure wish this damn leg would get better." Our prompting him to visit a doctor went unheeded.

The pain never left his leg and other pains became evident in his lower abdomen. This finally alerted him that something was definitely wrong and our prodding worked. He visited his company physician, and it was announced that they suspected ulcers. Ulcer medicines and diets were prescribed but after a couple of months, with no relief, he underwent tests at Deaconess Hospital, and was given a clean bill of health. This was during Thanksgiving weekend, 1955. However, a week or so later, Dad was again in so much pain that we took him to Cleveland Clinic, considered to be one of the best medical facilities in the world.

During exploratory surgery, and as Dad was coming out of the anesthesia, he heard the surgeons announce, "There it is. We found it!" He felt relief, he later told us, that finally there was an answer. If they found it, he was sure they could "fix it." Mom, Gerri and I were called in for a meeting with the clinic staff. We were told it was bone cancer. We were told that it had spread too far, and it was just a matter of time. They could do nothing to arrest the spreading disease.

Mother then had to go back into the hospital room to greet a waking Dad. He was upbeat and delighted that they had found the trouble. Mom did not tell him. She put on an acting performance as she told him she, too, was happy now that "they had found it." Inside, she was crushed. For the rest of her life, Mom claimed that she deserved the Academy Award — that no actress could have done a better job than she did at this most difficult moment. We never did share the impending "death sentence" with him, yet somehow I think he must have known. We brought him home where he stayed in a hospital bed in our living room since navigating stairs was difficult. On the 11th of February I went outside to get the morning newspaper as I always did. When the paper was not there, Dad's response was, "The damn paper boy is late again." He wanted to work his daily crossword puzzle. I began to prepare breakfast and take my insulin when I heard Dad make an unfamiliar snorting sound. I found him in a seated position in the hospital bed, appearing unconscious. I was right in his face calling "Dad Dad," to no reply or movement. I shook him by his shoulders. Still no movement. As unfamiliar as I was with mouth-to-mouth resuscitation, I attempted to do so, to no avail. I ran to the kitchen phone and dialed the number of the police station. Donna appeared on the staircase and I shouted to her to get back to her room. When Mom came downstairs she rushed to his side and hugged him. Gerri appeared and called Doctor Roenigk. Both women instinctively knew what I could not believe. Two police officers arrived and all they did was check for a pulse and peer into his eyes as they made Mom stand away. In what seemed like minutes, Doctor Straubs, an associate of Doctor Roenigk, arrived. While we stood motionless, with my little sister standing on the stairway, her brown eyes startled by and questioning everything, Doctor Straubs pronounced our father dead. As they took him out of our house, I did not cry; I told myself that it was not true; my dad is not going to die, not my Dad.

The doctors had given him six months but it took only two.

For me, it was the loss of not only my father, but my best friend. This is the man I sat with for hours, listening to his stories. The man who told me about life. This is the man who taught me how to swing a bat and throw a ball and every other thing I knew. This is the man who helped me with my homework. The man I golfed with and ate with. Who took me to work with him. The man who had measured my food and defended me as a lion would defend his cub. This is the man who let me play ball when I wasn't supposed to. This was the man who taught me about honesty and integrity, who taught me to control, not be controlled by, my diabetes. This was the loss of Dad.

It was difficult for the entire family, for each of us in our own way. Mom now had Donna to look after alone. She claimed that this helped her keep her feet on the ground. She eventually took a writing position with an architectural trade magazine. With Dad's passing, we were not financially well off as his insurance policy was not nearly what it should have or could have been, but that's the way it was and that's the way we accepted it. It was all right; Dad did all he could to make our home a happy one, and he did so with a flourish. His strength, his wisdom, his sense of humor, his caring inspired each of us, and instructed us in the value of family, togetherness and love. He was only 52 years old, much too early to leave. Much too early for me to inherit the gold ring bearing our initials.

And Dad didn't leave without another important gift to me. It was before he died, on the second Sunday of December, when I played in a championship football game. Before I left the house, from his hospital bed, Dad gave me a "football talk," wished me luck, and told me to bring home a winner. Dad and I knew that because I played both offense and defense, as was usual for players at that time, and did the kicking and punting, that I was going to be putting out a lot of energy. As always, I had my utility bag on the sidelines containing a thermos of sugar juice.

As half-time approached, I thought for sure I heard Dad's cough. Dad had a unique, recognizable cough. I could tell it apart from any other. It had a raspy, harsh sound. But it was okay, it was Dad's. I looked for him but with the chill in the air and the breath steam coming from the fans, plus my own, I could not locate him. I thought that it might be my imagination.

Then, at half time in the locker room, I almost lost it. Here comes Dad, as he always did. The coaches allowed him into the locker room during games mainly because of my diabetes. They knew that he knew better than anyone what kind of condition I was in. He was bundled in his winter coat, he had a scarf tied over his ears, under his ever-present felt hat. He walked slowly and was almost upon me when I saw him. I was shocked. Here was a man that could hardly walk, here was a man that just two weeks earlier, we were told, had three to six months to live. Here was a man that probably knew this would be the last game he would see his son play. Here was a man, my dad.

Dad came into that locker room, asked if I was okay, asked if I wanted his scarf to place under my shoulder pads on the left side where I had dislocated my shoulder two weeks earlier. As always, he wanted to be sure I had what I needed. As always, as he had done for so many years, he had that trusty canteen that was now so very old, but that contained his special mixture of orange juice and sugar, just in case.

Dad always made me feel that diabetes was never mine alone. It was as if he, and Mom, too, had diabetes. It was he who taught me to confront diabetes, and life, head on with determination yet with a serenity that comes from a resolved mind and a dedicated, optimistic spirit. It was he who taught me that diabetes was something to respect. Friends, our father was a wonderful man and the best dad a guy could ever wish for. His loss left a void that will never be filled.

The King of All Wing-Dings

If it is to be, it is up to me. Howard Ferguson

I took a job at Bond's Clothing Store on Cleveland's east side and was soon promoted to store management. Because I was wasting nearly three hours a day going to and from work, I decided to get my own apartment in nearby Mayfield Heights, only three miles away. I found an apartment on the second floor of a building that had business establishments (a beauty parlor, a pet store, etc.), on the street level. The second and third floors of this building had apartments, as well as medical and other professional offices. My apartment was at the top of the stairs, and just outside my entry door was a series of mailboxes for all the building occupants. There must have been at least twenty individual boxes, all neatly numbered in metal rows of five across. The postman's master key opened the entire metal front.

The apartment lay-out became a critical factor in my health one day. The entry door led into the hallway of the apartment, and from there, you needed to turn left or right to go anywhere. Turning left led to the living room and the kitchen. Turning right led to my bedroom. It was a well-maintained building and my living quarters were quite comfortable with a reasonable rental charge, perfect for a single guy.

One morning the alarm went off and I found myself in a hypoglycemic reaction, a good one! I was unable to turn off the alarm. My mind was perfectly clear but my sugar was so low that my movements were absolutely non-existent. My mind said, "Okay, Don, turn off the alarm," but my lack of any muscle control would not allow me to do so. After what I believe were several minutes, I began to rock my body in the bed. My concentration was at its strongest level as I knew I needed every possible effort to get that blankety-blank alarm clock turned off. The alarm sound was becoming a horrible, blaring sound that seemed like a freight train whistle, right in my ear. I don't know how long it took me to get my body on my side, but it seemed like an eternity. Now I could see the clock and my mind, still clear, knew it would be a continuing effort to reach it with my hand, to get it OFF. The terrible sound grew louder with each minute. I began talking to my hand and arm, "Come on, arm, move; Come on, hand, get over there and shut off that clock." I talked to them in my mind "Move, come on move." Finally, my arm reached over to the bedside table. I don't know if it was a reach or just a raise and fall onto the table. It did not matter, I was near the clock. Now to hit the turn-off button on the backside, a chore that would be more difficult than the other tasks. My hand and arm rested on that table as if they belonged to someone else. Neither would react to my wishes. More time elapsed until finally my arm twitched and I concentrated on getting it to move and, if nothing else, knock that clock from the table. Maybe with any luck the plug would pull from the wall or maybe it would break. Never had I wished so hard for something to break. At no time did I think I could not accomplish my task. Once again, the impact of the doctor twenty years earlier telling me "You can't" was translated into, "I will."

Little by little, my arm began to lurch in the direction of the screeching. Not smoothly, but in jerky motions, uncontrolled, as if my arm was filled with jumping beans. Lo and behold! My arm jumped, leaped and it hit that noisy clock and knocked it onto the floor. The off button must have bumped against something because a beautiful sound of peaceful quiet followed. The gentle sound of no sound at all was a tremendous relief.

Well, that part was over; now I had to get myself to the kitchen, way down at the other end of the hall. But first I had to get out of bed. Here we go again — now I'm on my side and I began rocking once more. My hand was still on the table and so with a little lunge of my spastic arm and my slow rocking movement, I got my 175 pounds to the floor, with an enormous thud.

Now, to get out of the room would take some crawling as there was no way I could stand. My legs lay at the end of my body like two worthless poles.

It was pure determination that propelled me to crawl, more like *drag* myself over the carpeted floor. I got to the hallway and began the longest "walk" of my life. The hallway appeared to be several football fields long. I later measured the hallway: 42 feet long. I finally got to the refrigerator. There was orange juice in the fridge, there was Pepsi Cola, there was food, there were several fresh fruits. This will be great. Not true, I could not get the refrigerator door open. I tried to reach it from my prone position, I tried to raise my body to touch the handle. I swung my arm at it, hoping to get lucky and hook my fingers on that handle. No such luck. Now what do I do? My mind kept thinking, ideas, ideas, ideas, what in the world am I going to do? The outside door, the entry door. Maybe if I can knock on the door, somebody in the hallway will hear me. That was my best thought. Crawl again, back over the portion I had crawled over before, but now I noticed it seemed a little easier. Maybe I was just getting into this crawling mode and had it mastered.

Reaching the door, I thumped, banged and hit the door with my hand, my arm and an occasional head butt. And then I heard a voice. The voice called in, "Is someone there?" My response was a garble of noise as speech was not possible. Just noises. "Are you all right?" the voice asked. Again, I grunted or slurred something. "Open the door," the voice demanded. "Open the door." Oh, brother, this will be a circus — I couldn't get that door open. A common, everyday door knob, but I could not turn it, not even grip it. I bumped and hit the door again and babbled some more.

In an instant, I heard the jingle of keys and saw the door knob turn. The door opened but my almost useless body lay directly in its path. An arm reached around and helped to move me as the door was pushed with more force. Two men entered. One, the postman who had heard my knocking, and the other, the building custodian who had the keys. The mailman realized something was wrong by the unusual sounds and requested help from the keeper of the keys. The custodian then went to one of the doctors' offices and a doctor and nurse arrived. Their second question was the important one, "Are you a diabetic?" My head nodded up and down with a yes motion. The doctor drew blood and my sugar level was at 67. They asked about orange juice in the refrigerator and again I nodded affirmative.

I really looked a sight. In the crawling and dragging, I scraped my knees, elbows and forearms raw. They were covered with blood. On my crawl back to the door, my T-shirt and undershorts picked up more blood. There was blood all over me and it certainly put a fright into the people that came to help. I realized why the return crawl was a bit less difficult — the blood on the carpet and my body helped me slide.

Diabetes can remind us every day that we can't do some action that others can do. That morning in my apartment served to show diabetes that we can. The human will is a powerful force.

At the time, I did not look at this event as a competition of any kind, but as the years passed, I came to realize it was possibly the most difficult competition I ever faced. In a sort of contest with myself, I was able to move my arm. It was sheer will that pulled me down that hallway. You can say it was sheer stubbornness that helped save my life.

And yes I learned something. Although I had always known I should check my urine twice a day for sugar content, this king of all wing-dings taught me that I MUST check my sugar three times a day, and definitely before going to bed.

By the way, my alarm was set for 7:30 and when I returned to my room to get ready for work, the clock read 9:45. I called in late for work that day.

Frances

*Good friends are hard to find, harder to leave,
and impossible to forget.* Anonymous

Following the wing-ding at my apartment, I moved into a room in a private home. The concern that this wing-ding created for my family and friends was so intense that I had to relocate to a place where someone would be able to keep an eye on me. I suppose this was as much for my own peace of mind as it was theirs.

Frances Walko was a widow whose husband had passed away some five years earlier, and her two children were married and living out of town. They had come to the United States prior to World War II from then-Czechoslovakia. She came to our house initially a few times a week to help Mom with Donna. The setting of her house in West Park Cleveland was ideally located half-way between my work and the ball parks where I spent much of my free time.

Her three-story house was tall and skinny. When I looked at it I always thought of the builder who must have known he was placing a house in a space that was not quite wide enough, but still he didn't want the lot to go to waste. Instead, he squeezed the house onto that small plot of land. Since Frances did not drive, I had use of the garage. The driveway was so narrow it was difficult to navigate without hitting the house. To complicate matters, the steep incline of the driveway made maneuvering up and down almost impossible during the winter months of ice and snow.

Frances, concerned about my well-being, acted almost like a mother to me. She frequently offered me dinner and I would share a meal with her. Her thick Slovak accent lent a colorful touch to the stories of Catholic saints she always told to me and to other visitors that dropped by for tea and homemade butter cookies. The stories were so real to her that she was able to tell them in a way that impressed me. We had heard no tales of saints from the pulpit of our Methodist church.

Our understanding was that if I did not awaken one morning, she would call the police station and officers would arrive to help. It would be a definite fact that if I did not arise after the alarm sounded, if I was covered with perspiration or acting unusual, I was having a wing-ding. If I was okay, I would immediately get out of bed to signal that all was well. (Rising quickly became a lifelong habit with me. My family tells me I am one of the "fastest risers" they know.) Prior to moving in with Frances, I visited the police station, just three blocks away, and met several of the officers — including Kelly and Jim — in that precinct. I explained that their assistance, if it was needed, would usually be in the morning hours. They understood my situation and seemed almost anxious to lend a hand

Their help was needed frequently because my eating habits were not as well regimented as they should have been. With my activities in sports almost year-round, I often allowed a full meal to escape me. With working on one side of Cleveland and my athletic activities on the other, I would have a milkshake and a hamburger instead of meat, potatoes, vegetables, milk and an apple or other fresh fruit. If we were scheduled for an early game, 6:30 or 6:45, I didn't make ample time to work a full day, run to my room or a men's room to change into whatever uniform was necessary that particular day, and then drive to the game. It was irresponsible behavior on my part and a milkshake will never be prescribed on a diabetic's menu. This, too, became part of my learning the importance of discipline in controlling my diet.

I would, however, always make certain that I had my "juice jug," or buy a Pepsi or Orange drink at the refreshment stand, add sugar, and then keep it near the bench area. My teammates knew that these beverages were my "medicine," and I cannot recall anyone ever drinking it or even taking a sip. Due to my poor eating habits and my running lower than usual on sugar because of all the exercise, Frances probably needed to call the police station an estimated ten times in the 13 or 14 months I lived with her. In each situation, I would be completely asleep, or more than likely, unconscious. As I remember, officers Kelly and Jim were there each time as they were on the morning shift. It was on one of these mornings that I punched Jim in the forehead.

After I moved away from Frances, Jim and I continued to see each other in football stadiums during the season. I learned that Jim played in the same football league on an opposing team. We often related to one of the visits that he and Kelly had made while my sugar level was low.

For years, as a gesture of thanks to Frances, not a Christmas went by that Mom, poinsettia in hand and with my kid sister in tow, did not visit Frances at her tall, skinny house. Frances then had a new member of our family to fascinate with the stories of martyrs and saints, and to stuff with tea and butter cookies. Our family's relationship continued with Frances into the 1980s. We discovered later that Frances had gone into a Catholic nursing home where she continued to live for many years. Heaven must by now be a place tailor-made for Frances.

7
Family

When you love, your actions and words should be windows of your heart. DWR

Penny's From Heaven

Bond's Clothing Store turned out to be one of the most important jobs I ever had. That is where I met Penny. Actually, I met her twice. Once during my two and one-half years as manager, and again when I returned to Bond's, part-time.

Penny was a teenager in high school when she worked as a part-time office employee. I was twenty and since I worked at one of the suburban stores and she at the main store, I would see her only occasionally. She was a very attractive girl, but nonetheless, a "kid" of 16.

By the Christmas season of 1957, Penny had graduated from high school, had another full-time job, and remained in her part-time position at Bond's. This time, when I arrived at the store, the first person to capture my eye was Penny Barker. Wow, did she catch my eye. She was now 19 and beautiful. I was 23, and the age difference didn't seem all that important anymore.

I approached her almost as quickly as I could get my coat hung up and spoke with her briefly. I then asked if I could take her to a movie or to dinner one evening of the upcoming week. She didn't answer immediately, but when I asked again several days later, she accepted.

Our first time together was when I asked if I could drive her home after work. I knew she took a bus to and from work, but I never had asked where she lived. As we walked toward the car, I asked where her home was. "Mentor," she replied. When I first heard, "Mentor," I shuddered because I knew this small town was thirty miles east of the store and a one hour car ride. I lived 15 miles west of the store, but I carried on as if it didn't matter. Anyway, she was pretty enough, and so I made the drive. As our relationship grew, the drive to see her, to court her, was more like a tour to paradise. Her beauty, her figure, her personality, intelligence and grace were more than any man deserves.

That was about 45 years ago. We were married on September 20, 1958. Today, I still find my wife one of the most beautiful women in the world. There is a song that questions, "Do I love you because you're beautiful, or are you beautiful because I love you?" My answer is yes to both. This book is dedicated to many people, but none is more honored than my marvelous wife. Penny has experienced so many different aspects of me and my diabetes that she deserves medals of valor and medals for patience. She has been with me for three-quarters of my sixty-plus diabetic years. She has courageously been through each and every experience that was placed before us. She has mastered living with this ailment as much as I have. For this alone, she is remarkable.

There were times a particular wing-ding was difficult for Penny. There were times she had to call for help to get me out of a low sugar situation, times she had to explain to people, to policemen, that I was diabetic. There were times she felt my sports should be more limited, and times she felt that I should quit these activities altogether. Her thoughts

Penny and Don Ray

were: fewer sports, fewer reactions. She never winced at the needles I had to use and never seemed to mind my taking injections. She seemed to take pride in preparing delicious meals. Had I not been a diabetic and had I not been as involved in sports, Penny would have liked it better.

But I believe by far, the good has overshadowed the bad.

When Don asked me if I would please write a couple of paragraphs for his book, I thought I couldn't possibly do that. I felt I had certain negative feelings that would be out of place in an otherwise positive story. I was afraid I would feel like a hypocrite to write about only the good things in our lives. After all, the diabetes has been a handful. Often I've thought I'm the one who should write the book.

On many occasions I have had to be concerned for his health and his safety. I recall one incident when he didn't come home from work at his usual time, and didn't call. I knew something was wrong. I called the police and had them search for him. Our children were young at the time and we were a one-car family. A few worry-filled hours later, it occurred to me that I had not checked the garage as I would usually have heard him pull in the driveway. Well, there he was, sound asleep in the car, having a low blood sugar reaction.

Reading his manuscript helped me to realize something important: I need not dwell on the isolated incidences that made me worry and fret, or that caused me to be sick to my stomach. Instead, I need to concentrate on the overall picture of our lives. I decided I could indeed contribute by providing the spouse's side of the story.

For some unknown reason, I am much more astute than Don at predicting an insulin reaction. I can sense when he is two floors away that his blood sugar is starting to get low. When I am downstairs, for instance, and he is upstairs in our tri-level house, I can tell just by the way he moves that a wing-ding is beginning. The sound of his steps or the rhythm of his walk may be "off." At *night when in bed, it may be an unusually heavy snoring that wakes me. I'll touch him and know immediately that he needs glucose. He is wet from perspiration and his skin is clammy. He is in a deep reaction. Sometimes his wing-dings in the early states leave him indecisive, unable to make a decision at that moment. If he needs to reach for a candy bar or pour a drink of juice, he often seems unable or unwilling to do so. It is as if the lack of sugar has translated into a lack of calories and slowed down his brain and other bodily functions.*

Don believes he can "feel" it when his blood sugar is too high or too low and that he "catches" it before it goes too far. Often this is true, but again, often this is not true. Originally, his parents, his family members and former teammates were first to notice a change in his behavior signaling a hypoglycemic reaction. I have been in the position of primary "catcher" on this behavioral team!

If I know Don needs some sugar I will never quite understand why he also doesn't know each and every time. I sometimes wonder if he just refuses to accept that fact. It may be a type of denial that I believe most diabetics and their families face. It may be similar to the denial an alcoholic experiences when the family hears, "I don't have a problem."

Most of the information in Don's manuscript was not new to me; however, what I learned from it were many of Don's inner feelings, of which I was not totally aware. This references his years of growing up and the emotional struggles. Fortunately in his case, he had a wonderful family to carry him through those difficult times. I am concerned about diabetics, especially children, who have no others to care for and support them as completely.

Don is the first to tell you that he is one of the luckiest men alive. Don and I are humbled and blessed by all the good people in this world who have come forward to help him, wanting nothing in return. A true story exemplifies his good fortune.

Several decades ago, Don was alone on a long drive across town in the early hours when a reaction set in. He had the good sense to pull over to the side of the road, but then could not move his muscles to help himself. Fortunately, a newspaper boy walking down this road saw him behaving oddly, and rather than continuing on his way, approached the car. Don could not talk but motioned toward the medical alert necklace that is always a part of his attire. This necklace was purchased for him years earlier by his older sister. The car door was unlocked. Had it been locked, Don would have been unable to open it. The news carrier was able to read the message the necklace provided. Now knowing that this man was diabetic and sugar was necessary, he went away and returned with candy bars. Don later explained that he never realized how difficult it was to chew peanuts, but chew he did because they were mixed in the chocolate bar. He recovered quickly and offered to pay the young man for the sweets, but he refused.

Wing-dings occurred from time to time. When Don comes out of a reaction it seems to me that he is even better than he normally would be. There seems to be a euphoria associated with the recovery. He also recovers rapidly. It is I who am left with the after effects of a wing-ding.

Now here is the greatly overshadowing good side. No woman on this earth has been loved more by her husband than I. His love is unconditional. A romantic? Yes! I have stacks of poetry that he has written to me over the years. I have had to be very careful about ever commenting that I like something because if I do, it will soon be mine. He has always liked surprising me with gifts and trips. And little things — on any given night I might pull into the garage from work and find a huge, handwritten sign, "Dinner and a movie?"

Don always says in a marriage that you have to give more than 50% and that you need to overlap. Well, he's a 75 percenter! I believe because of his medical background that he has strong feelings to live for today because none of us know what tomorrow may bring.

I would like to mention one thing at this point. I always hear about diabetics having big mood swings. This may be true for many, but Don is a very even-keeled person. He rarely shows anger and wakes up singing in the mornings. He is always ready for any type of social activity. Not once in more than four decades have I ever heard him say, "No, I don't feel like doing that or going there." He has loved and supported our children and their families. He loved our dog.

The only thing I would change about our life is to have had more information about Type 1 diabetes. If treatment information was available, we were not in the loop to receive it, especially after Dr. Roenigk left private practice. Though we probably should have sought out a support group or been more active with the Juvenile Diabetes Foundation, we never gave it a thought. We also did not have access for years to the at-home diagnostic equipment or the glucose gels that are now available.

Other than that, I wouldn't have changed my life for anything or anyone. Thank you, Don, for all the loving years. I love you!

Penny

Our Kids

We were married almost three years before we had our first of four children, all diabetes free. Our concerns that Penny was not pregnant sooner took me to Doctor Roenigk, but some simple tests revealed that my diabetes was not a factor and we were likely to become parents. Four months after those tests, it was confirmed that Penny was pregnant. Dawn Marie was born on March 7, 1961.

Scott, Dawn, Sheila, Debby

I never thought of NOT having children. For Penny and me, it was never an issue of whether to have children, but rather, how many. The number four worked out as we had hoped. Doctor Roenigk assured us that there wouldn't be any complications. Dawn was such a delight that we were pleased to welcome Sheila 16 months later. As a rule, Sheila and I celebrate our birthdays on July 4th, the day in between our birthdays. My birthday cakes have always been low sugar, angel food cakes. Debby, our youngest daughter, was born quite a few years later, in 1967. She and my mother always celebrated their October birthdays together. Another nine years would pass before we had our son.

Scott was born in 1976. On July 17, Dawn worked as a teen assistant aide at Fairview Hospital when Penny arrived there to deliver. She wheeled her mother to the maternity ward, not by walking, but by jumping, prancing and joyously announcing greetings to anyone that would listen that her baby brother was about to be born.

Dawn became the leader of the Ray children, always the one her siblings looked to for guidance and advice. She was a leader in school and active in the student foreign exchange program. She had the good fortune to spend a year in Japan. Before she left, she did not speak the language, but by her return, spoke fluent Japanese and wrote it proficiently. That year, she was selected the outstanding foreign exchange student in Japan. She remains in close contact with her Japanese "family" and had the opportunity to take her oldest child, daughter Noelle, to visit them. Her two sons may yet have the privilege. Dawn is a homemaker and a sometimes entrepreneur. She is quite a woman.

Dawn and her husband David, as well as my daughter Sheila and her husband Jim live in a nearby suburb of Cleveland.

Sheila became our ballerina and attended the Cleveland School of Ballet. She was voted Homecoming Queen during her senior year at Fairview High School and was a member of the dance drill team that entertained at athletic events. Before becoming a wife and mother, Sheila held an executive secretarial position. She diligently helped me type, from cassette tape, the first draft of this book! Since then she gave birth to four children within three years, which includes a set of twins. In addition to her capabilities as a home manager, she has an outstanding talent for interior decorating and home design. She continues to teach ballet part-time and will always be my prima ballerina.

Debby has kept us entertained and laughing. Her sense of humor is unique in the world, and she has the ability to mimic. Debby lives in Columbus with her husband John and two little girls. All my kids, as well as my sister Donna, graduated from Fairview Park High. Debby played on the school's State Championship Volleyball Team and continued volleyball throughout her education at Muskingum College. Her senior year, Debby was selected one of the best defensive volleyball players in the nation, receiving NCAA recognition. Debby wore #5 on her uniform in her four years at high school and her four years at college in recognition of my lifelong baseball number. She honored me in so doing. In fact, there had never been a #5 on Muskingum's volley ball team until Debby's request.

Scott never suffered as the result of being younger brother to three sisters, and, if anything, I believe his respect for women in general deepened because of it. Scott was a three-sport guy at Fairview, featuring football and baseball. While at Muskingum, he lettered four years in football as a fullback. Scott was voted captain in his senior year, and received a Most Valuable Player award. Scott wore #34 all through high school and college in recognition of two professional players, Walter Payton and Kevin Mack, as well as an outstanding high school athlete he admired, Paul Maleski. Scott took advantage of his double major in International Business and Spanish by spending a year overseas as an assistant professor at the University of Toledo in Spain. He is presently single and is employed with Moen Faucet Company in a sales and marketing position for Latin America at their U.S. headquarters located a few miles from where we live. Scott has visited many countries in Europe and has been to Mexico. He never ceases to amaze me with his ever-expanding knowledge.

These "kids" are a joy to be around. Not only are they fun, but in addition, they are deep thinkers, ready for a philosophical discussion and good debate, especially with each other. Each of my four children can share a situation with my diabetes that presented itself. I cannot tell you the number of times that they had to help me through a wing-ding by seeing warning signs prior to a reaction, and bringing me orange juice or something sweet to bring my sugar level back to normal.

As horrific as these stories may seem, they were the exception to our usual daily life.

I've asked each of my children to relay a memory of their life with my diabetes. Below are the incidents they recall, along with their thoughts.

D awn shares a story during her sophomore year when I had picked her up from high school. On the short drive home, I had a hypoglycemic reaction. Dawn insisted that I stop driving and pull over to the curb. She recalls that I was somewhat obstinate about it but I did comply, just four blocks from home. We had no sugar, candy or glucose in the car, as we usually do. On her insistence, I slid over on the bench seats to the passenger side of the car. Being resourceful, she drove the car home. She had me stay in the car until she returned with a glass of sugar-juice. Her learner's permit required her to be accompanied by an adult while driving. She felt she was not breaking any of the rules as her father was with her.

I have countless childhood memories of my dad. And, yes, the diabetes did play a role in those memories. There was the time in mid-winter, clad only in slippers and a robe, that I ran to a neighbor's house to get help because my father was having an insulin reaction. (It was years before I came to know that "wing-dings" were not a scientific term!) There was the time we were at the airport with our friends from Japan when Dad had a wing-ding. Once, when we were house hunting, he was on the verge of a reaction and we abruptly pulled into a restaurant so he could eat.

Growing up, our summers were filled with fun. Baseball was our religion. The baseball field was the altar and the stands were pews filled with *his adoring fans, his family. Dad played, managed and coached baseball as far back as I can remember. And, he was good! He was the best. If you needed a hit to right to score a run, he was your man. In my eyes, he was like a god on that baseball field.*

To every game, Dad brought a glass peanut butter jar which he had refurbished into a thermos. This makeshift thermos was completely covered in masking tape except for a long, narrow window so that he could see how much was left. How much what was left? Orange juice, ice and a few extra heaping spoonfuls of sugar graced the inside of that peanut butter jar. We always wanted to sneak little sips from this forbidden chalice, but we knew Dad needed his spruced-up orange juice in case his sugar got low. All the baseball guys teased him about what secret concoction he really had in there, which was ironic because the stiffest drink Dad ever had was a Pepsi, straight up.

I firmly believe my father leads a totally normal life, spiked with insulin reactions. He has proven time and time again his resilience and his ability to turn the Cannot Do's into the Can Do's. Despite diabetes in the family, we children had the most "normal" all-American upbringing you could ask for. Today, I recognize the miracle of his living "symbiotically" with diabetes for more than sixty years. I adore my dad.

Dawn Ray Filippi

*wing-ding (n) - our family name for a hypoglycemic reaction. Symptoms include: shaking, sweating profusely, drooling, foaming at the mouth, gritting of the teeth, a seemingly drunken appearance, a coma-like state, and obstinacy.

S heila recalls a wing-ding that was memorable to her when she was about eight years old. I was driving home from work and had a low sugar reaction. The police stopped me and arrested me for "intoxication." When she found out that the police had her father in custody, she thought I was going to jail for life. She was horrified and began to imagine what life would be without her father. Penny must have told them over the telephone that I was diabetic, though we would all like to think the officers checked my wallet for my medical card or looked at my ever-present identification necklace. It would have helped if that had been done before they arrested me! Even now, thirty years later, Sheila confesses that this was one of the most frightening times of her life.

I *suppose I always took my father and his diabetes for granted. I never realized this until Dad's 65th surprise birthday party. Everybody who spoke about him that night spoke about his being a diabetic. This intrigued me. I had never thought of it as such a big deal. Growing up with my dad's disease, I knew no differently. Diabetes was part of him; Dad and diabetes went hand-in-hand. His condition was not earth shattering to me. He was able to manage it. I was probably too close to this condition to see it for the dangerous disease that it could be. This is how I felt up until this party when a light went on for me as I listened to friends and relatives. This was a big deal! It was earth shattering that my father had this disease. I already knew how lucky I was to still have him around at age 65, but never had I taken into account how incredibly fortunate I was to have my Diabetic Dad around at age 65. At that moment, I realized what a remarkable man he is, in every way.*

Growing up with a diabetic parent taught me to stay calm during crisis situations. It taught me to be sympathetic yet strong with someone in need. Living with my father taught me to never give up hope for anything. My father is my hero.

Sheila Ray Buckingham

Debby tells the story of coming home from elementary school one spring afternoon to find me sound asleep on the floor of our family room. She knew immediately that I was in the midst of a deep reaction. I refer to this as a "deep" reaction as I had apparently been asleep and in a low-sugar state for quite some time as I was, she reports, soaking wet from perspiration and thrashing about. I did not respond to her pleading for me to awake. She knew the ritual of orange juice with sugar or something sweet. When she could not get me to respond, she went to our neighbors who called the emergency medical team that arrived to administer glucose. Debby says that because she was the only one at home, this was a frightening moment for her. I imagine it would be to most 11-year olds. Our neighbors have experienced several situations where they were called upon for assistance over the years. A special thanks to them all and to the Glovers and the Zullis, our good neighbors for nearly thirty years.

Oh, my dad is diabetic? Of course, I know he is, but I never felt that I had a father with limitations because of it. I watched Dad play sports and perform physical labor. He ran alongside me while teaching me to ride a bike and taught me how to slide into a base and hit a softball.

Having a diabetic father has meant different things to me over the years. When I was a child, it meant he had to take shots, keep candy on hand, (Chuckles was a favorite) and make sure he had enough orange juice in his jug for softball games. His diabetes was never put in a negative light. Sure there were wing-dings and some would really scare me, but they were infrequent and quickly passed.

Now that I am an adult, I am aware of the complications that could arise because of the diabetes. There have been times when I wished Dad wasn't diabetic, but I have NEVER heard him wish it, even when directly asked. It's just another part of him: his eyes are green, he talks a lot, and he's diabetic. It's just another piece of the puzzle that makes him who he is. That, I wouldn't change for anything.

It is my father's unwavering positive attitude towards living with diabetes that gives me comfort. I've been told I have the same positive outlook on life. I've learned over the years that should my children have diabetes, I already know that they could attend dance class, play sports, get married and have a family someday. I've seen my father live that life. I am so proud to be his daughter.

I love you, Dad.

Debby Ray Molino

Scott can tell his story of a low blood sugar reaction that happened not long ago. He had graduated from college and I had a wing-ding while in our family room lounge chair. It was about 1:00 AM and I had fallen asleep and into a very deep reaction, one of the most severe that I have experienced. Generally

Penny can take control and bring me through, but neither he nor Penny could get me out of this one. Scott called our local emergency unit and they responded in a few minutes. As is routine, they monitored my sugar level prior to treatment. It registered at 56. A normal range for most diabetics is 90 to 120 or a little higher. Normal for me is a reading of 105 to 110. Scott commented that he hopes he never sees one comparable to that again. I had been extremely active that day which affected my blood sugar and had a lot to do with the episode.

The only way to look at my father and his relationship with diabetes is as a success story. This is a disease that is one of the leading causes of death in the United States, and he has lived with it, relatively complication free, for more than 60 years. He is a trailblazer, as were my grandparents, in facing life with diabetes. They were told he would be blind at the age of 50, that he couldn't play sports and would probably have an amputation at some point during his "short" life.

He was not dealt a perfect hand, but he has played the cards that he was given as best as he possibly could. In poker, you can win even if you don't have a royal flush or four of a kind. This depends on the skill with which you play the game, and on a little luck. In the card game of life, my father has had a little of both. He got a bad card in Diabetes, but he hasn't let that stop him from winning the game.

Our family never doubted that he was winning all the way. In fact, none of my siblings nor I realized, as we were growing up, the seriousness of diabetes. It wasn't until we were adults and we read the manuscript of this book that we learned about the tough tribulations that can come from diabetes. I don't want to give the impression that we didn't know our father had a disease, but we didn't realize the extent of what diabetes could do. We knew diabetes as our father taking shots every morning with the regularity of the sunrise, and giving him a glass of sugared orange juice when he was acting strange. Diabetes seemed simple to us because he has been lucky enough to never have any serious complications. He has been able to take advantage of that luck because he has, with the help of his loved ones around him, taken care of himself. He has stayed active, taken his shots every day, kept his sugar counts and never neglected his health and needs for nutrition.

This does not explain it all, however. The most important thing in both his winning with diabetes, and our relatively simplistic understanding of diabetes is his attitude. I have never heard him complain. He merely says that God gave him diabetes because he was strong enough to handle it. He has a sense of humor about it all, too. For example, he gave his hypoglycemic reactions that playful name of "wing-ding."

My father is the glue of our entire family. He loves nothing more than to have us together. Any time I've ever needed him, whether it be supporting me at a football game, a concert, a play, or helping me when I'm in trouble, he's always been there for me. It would have been a shame if diabetes kept him from doing those beautiful things that only a father can do. I will always hold the memory of the Muskingum football game when it was so freezing cold that spectators left to go home, players on the bench were excused, and the band left the field, but when I looked into the stands, Dad was still there. If his son was in the game, so was he.

Still, we've each had to deal with the harsh realities of diabetes. There is always an underlying fear that an injury or wound could turn into something worse for Dad, but he has made it this far without any problems. I've seen him in some scary states, sweating profusely, foaming from the mouth, in a seizure-like trance with lifeless eyes, as if he has gone to a totally different world. I've seen him in a nearly violent or abusive state. The majority of the time, when in a wing-ding, he just acts silly, as though he is drunk. These are the lighter reactions that are sometimes pretty comical. I consider these to be a trade-off because he does not drink. I'd take my dad's occasional goofy actions over some drunk's any day.

Dad has undoubtedly won his game with diabetes. He has maintained a high level of activity for years. He was playing softball in highly competitive leagues into his late forties. I remember going with him to his basketball league every Saturday when he was in his fifties. The other players in their thirties were heard making typical complaints about how they just can't keep up like they used to. I've never heard these words, or anything similar, spoken by my father. He just ran up and down the floor in the full enjoyment and appreciation of the ability to compete, and made his presence known with his aggressive defense.

Living with my father has taught me not to take any of my abilities for granted. Through him I learned to recognize how lucky I am and not to *waste my God-given gifts. There were supposed to be times that he couldn't do something because of diabetes, but he never bothered to listen. He just became hungrier and more appreciative to do them. I learned that if I want something with an equal hunger, I, too can achieve my goal. He continues playing, living and loving, and for that, and so much more, I love him.*

Scott

Values and Traditions

Don Ray, Happy 65th Birthday!

Don, thank you for:
Showing me what it means to be extended family
that's really family,
Letting me know that if I called for help,
you'd be there no matter what,
Showing me how to walk a ladder,
Teaching me how to be positive about the future
and not complain about the past,
Showing me that people can have the courage to always
do what they feel is right,
Showing me how to combine an intense desire to win
with good sportsmanship.
In short, for showing me how to be
the kind of person I want to be.
Let this birthday celebration mark the first
day of a remarkable second half!

Roger Barker, Brother-in-Law
July, 1998 on the occasion of Don's surprise party

It is beyond extraordinary to see my children, all in the adult phase of their lives, so very close, giving to and caring for each other, helping one another, socializing with each other, watching each other's children when needed and simply getting along so well. Even in their adolescent years, the togetherness was obvious. This closeness has carried over to our nine grandchildren as whenever they are together, all nine or just a part of that total, there is a kind of rhythm that sets in and I see and hear my family's harmony. I hope they continue on the path that Penny and I hopefully help set for them, a path that is straight and true.

I believe the values and traditions generated by Mom and Dad, as well as those created on Penny's side of the family are a factor in our children's successes. Penny's mother, Blondena, and the rest of the Barker clan are also close knit with Penny's three brothers and one sister very much like my three daughters and one son. The difference is the male to female ratio. I too, have a marvelous relationship with my two sisters, both of whom now live in other states. Still, we manage to see each other once a year. My sister Gerri had four children who grew up with and have remained close to our kids, their cousins.

I sometimes wonder if the diabetes that God chose to let me have in some way had an effect on my children's caring, giving attitudes. It is true that their father had an ailment that many people looked upon as devastating, and that did, from time to time, give them something to face that never confronted their friends. How did the occasional reaction, the making sure the insulin was not forgotten when going out to dinner or to a picnic affect them? Did they watch as closely as their mother to be certain their dad was okay? Was this a part of their understanding and caring that stayed with them throughout their

A healthy next generation continues into the Millennium; our nine grandchildren — as of October, 2001. Top row, left to right in matching sweaters, Tristan, Geordon and Evan Buckingham, next to sister Alexa, surround their cousin Nick Filippi. They overlook Noelle and Mitchell Filippi and cousins Emily and Morgan Molino.

lives? Was my diabetes a little part of my children's learning process of togetherness, of pulling together whenever and wherever help or assistance was needed?

I suppose these questions can never be properly answered as there is no way they can be accurately measured. It is a definite fact that my diabetic condition was a part of their lives, but I do not believe it was a detriment or harmful in any way. I believe it helped to make us closer. I believe that the impact that diabetes had on their young lives is still apparent today in that closeness. I do not treat this fact of diabetes as a negative. It can be looked upon as a positive!

To demonstrate this, I look at these four adults and see what fine human beings they have become. Often the term success is used in relating to the world of work, to the world of money and finances. If one is successful it has meant that one is financially well-off. Each of my children is successful in the financial scheme of things, but success to us has always been determined in the ways of life, relationships with others, attempting to do what is right, cherishing a true friend and loving the family. My children have all excelled in this part of life's success, an accomplishment Penny and I consider far more important than financial prosperity alone. They are becoming, as Penny and I have become, multimillionaires in values and relationships.

When they were young, we went everywhere together, including my ball games. Penny and my girls were, without question, my biggest fans. When Scott joined the family, I was 42 years old. By the time he was old enough to understand baseball, I was pushing 50 and my skills had diminished and the competition was not as fierce. At that time I was playing because of the love I had for the game.

By the time the girls reached junior high, Penny and I taught them what to expect when they became interested in boys. It was evident that this was inevitable, and not too far off. We covered many things about life, and things they would be confronted by as they became young women. We touched strongly on how they should be treated when on a date with a young man. I, as their father, took the girls on "dates" when they were 12 or 13, and treated them as they should expect to be treated on a date. We would go to a movie and dinner — just me and one of my "little" girls.

When they were in high school and young men were driving, the girls would never leave the house unless their date approached and knocked on the front door; there would be no horn beeping from the driveway. This was the late '70s and early '80s and young men were expected to open all doors, but if not, my girls were instructed to stand at the doors until they did. No phone calls after 11:00 PM and never would they call a boy on the telephone. If a boy asked for a date, it had to be a week or five days in advance. Curfew was set at specific times and it was a must that the curfew be honored. The times would become later as they grew older.

On "our dates" I always made it a point to help them with their coats and their chairs and show respect, treating them as ladies. This had all been passed on to me by Mom and Dad, and I just followed their lead when guiding my three daughters.

With Scott, it was much the same but from the male side of the courtship. Some of the guidelines passed on to Scott were as follows: always be prompt, follow the girl's father's wishes, do not "beep" from the car, go to the front door, open doors wherever you might be, excuse yourself if you must leave the table or otherwise leave her presence, respect her femininity, protect her from harm and always treat each young lady as if she were a princess; treat her as if she were a breakable china doll. Respect and dignity were a must. With Scott, I always ended these comments as my father had to me: "If the young lady does not deserve that sort of treatment, then do not date her."

Although Scott did not have "a date" with Penny in the same way that the girls did with me, he took my mother, whom the kids called Nana, on a dinner date when he was only ten years old. It was 1986 and an early celebration for Nana in advance of her 80th birthday. The selected restaurant was crowded on their chosen evening, reservations were behind and the Maitre D' seated them a few tables away from the lounge area. After a few minutes, Scott decided that being seated "in the bar" was not the proper place for his grandmother and promptly requested of the Maitre D' to seat them in the main dining area. Nana told this story to anyone she would meet.

The Loss of Mom

Advancing age and several broken hips never stopped Mom as she went everywhere with her "walker," a four-legged cane on wheels. I don't know if Mom learned her tenacious attitude from me or if I learned it from her but she always said, "With my walker, I can go to the moon." Off she would go, impeccably dressed every day, to the grocery store, to the nursing home to volunteer, or to the department store to browse or shop.

Mom continued her work for the magazine until in the mid-'60s when she remarried. Her life then turned to women's club events and raising funds for scholarships and charities. Her health was quite good except for slight osteoporosis, a bit of arthritis and an angina condition of the heart. She had had several attacks of angina, but the paramedics and a visit to the hospital always put her back on track. She had an active life and at age 82 was even in the St. Patrick's Day Parade, waving from the stagecoach representing the nursing home where she volunteered. In the winter of 1987, however, one angina "attack" was quite different from the others and, with Gerri and me at the same hospital where all my kids were born, our Mom and Nana left us on December 12. She is buried, of course, next to Dad at Sunset Memorial Cemetery.

As was the case with Dad, I was the last one to speak with Mom. She had called 911 on her own and when the hospital notified me, I was there within minutes. Mom and I had time alone for awhile. She told me that she was afraid and I attempted to ease her fears. When they wheeled her away, I told her, "I will see you later." Yes, Mom, I will be there a little later.

Mom, you will be glad to know that Gerri was our strength, the guardian angel of the entire family throughout the "arrangements" and the initial stages of our grief. You will be glad to know it, but not surprised — it is something Gerri would do.

Penny tells me that on occasion after Mom left us, I would cry in my sleep.

I may still.

My "Other Family"

There's the family that you're born with and another one you choose. Anonymous

From time to time, the athletic director of Fairview High would ask me to speak with one of the athletic students one-on-one. They may have been involved in a drinking incident or were having problems with grades. Although I never have had any formal training in the arena of counseling, I have listened to and learned from coaches all my life, and I felt that my association with young people over the years made it acceptable for me to speak with them. As a friend, an outsider, not a teacher or parent, I would meet with students and talk about the situation that suspended them, held them back in school or made them ineligible for sports.

To a young "drinker," I would say:

With modern medicine allowing a young person like yourself to live longer than your parents' generation, your life expectancy is close to 90 years of age. You are in your teens. I have often wondered why youngsters, like yourself, can't at least wait until they are 20 years old to begin drinking beer and wine. You will be drinking for 70 years. Isn't that long enough?

To the students slacking on grades, I would present their lives as sectioned into thirds. If they, like every one, were to look at their lives, they would see them sectioned into:

I. Personal hygiene
2. Fun and Play Time
3. Work and School Time

If you look at your week, you have 168 hours in a week with one-third of them, or 56 hours, for each of the above portions of your life. Part 1, Personal Hygiene, is where you sleep, bathe, eat, comb your hair, brush your teeth and so forth. Part 2 is where you play ball, go to a movie, take a part-time job, watch TV, hang around with your friends, go shopping and things of that nature. Part 3 takes us to work or school. Of these 56 hours related to school, you will spend 25 hours a week with five subjects of importance each day. You have another five hours of miscellaneous classes. That's a total of 30 hours. We'll add another five hours for lunch and study hall, which gives us a 35-hour total.

This means 21 hours are left. If you remove eight of those hours and sprinkle them into category one and two, it still leaves you with 13 hours. That's 13 hours each week unspoken for. That is 13 hours that if allocated to schoolwork and if you honestly spent that time on your homework, it is a guaranty that your grades will improve greatly and a failing mark will never again show up on your report card!

M y "other kids" have been the young people that have come in and out of my life: the boys I've coached, the girls I've coached, the kids I've talked to, not only about athletics, but about life.

I also have an extended, other "family." They are the good friends I've made over the years. Some I met at American Greetings Corp. where I worked for 37 years.

It was the first of March, 1971, that I started employment at American Greetings Corp.

During that first month, some folks learned I had played baseball at Kent State and introduced me to Don Ray. My financial services department and his chain sales department were right next to each other. Don was a player-coach for a slow-pitch team in the community where I lived with my new bride. Don asked if I would be interested in playing on his softball team. That was the beginning of a 30-year friendship.

My hometown was in New York and I didn't have a clue about the Cleveland area. Only twelve years my senior, Don became my dad away from home. He took me under his proverbial wing. He taught me things such as how to file income tax, and purchase a first home (he subsequently helped with a couple of others); he showed me the ropes at work, introduced me to many of his friends that today I can thankfully call my friends, too. We went to Browns games, Indians games, card games and parties. Don provided me with opportunities and pathways to take which enabled me to be a better father, husband, worker, coach, player, friend and caring person.

Don and Penny are the Godparents to our only child, Carie. The Rays are as fine a wholesome American family as you can find.

With regard to Don being a diabetic, I relay this short story: I was telling my now 27 year old daughter that Don was in the process of having a book published about his life with sugar diabetes, and that he had asked me to write a few words about our experiences. Carie's reaction: "Dad, I didn't know that Don has sugar diabetes." That *tells it all. As close as our families have been, Carie never knew. It was a non-issue. To those of us who are close to him, it doesn't exist because he doesn't dwell on it as a negative.*

Don Ray's legacy very well could be that of a self-taught teacher. He may never have been a school teacher, but let me tell you, the educational system missed a perfect teacher. He cares so much about people, young and old. Don has a way of inspiring and motivating and he knows how to communicate. He asked me to help him coach baseball or softball 5th grade boys to 9th grade girls and I watched him teach them all the facets of the game. I am certain they would tell you that they learned some principles of life as well. As a leader and an athlete on the field and off, he was outstanding. He is not average at anything I am aware of.

I have seen Don over the years overcome many medical problems. A few years ago, a broken hip and before that the car accident that would have killed most. Believe me, when I saw him in that hospital and even back at home, I had my doubts. When I left his home one night I said to Judy, my wife of 15 years, that I hope that's not the last time I see him alive; he looked that bad. The guy is as tough as they come, and you'd better not tell him that he can't, because I bet he will.

Don has made the best of his life by using a positive attitude and having lots of friends and a loving family backing him in every step he took or takes. I'm more than glad to be able to call him one of my closest friends.

Barry Cole

8
Coach

Sports not only build character, they reveal it.
Anonymous

Football is a very simple game to play.
On offense you knock somebody down.
And on defense, you knock somebody down.
DWR

In baseball, there are only two places
to pitch the ball: to the Catcher's left knee
and to the Catcher's right knee.
Bob Walton, coach

It's often easy to win the easy game
and often hard to win the tough games.
The trick is to make every game easy.
DWR

When a pitched ball is eye high, it is too high.
DWR

When I listened to every word and watched every move of my father, I was learning to coach. As years passed, I gained knowledge, insight, thoughts and mannerisms from many coaches.

Bob's Story

*Don't look down on someone unless you're
helping that someone up.* Anonymous

About a year after the coma, Bob, our neighbor,
asked me to teach him how to throw and catch
a ball. The son of our next-door neighbors whom
we loving called Aunt Ruth and Uncle Bill, Bob was
ten years my senior. He also had Muscular
Dystrophy. From his early childhood, the muscles
in his upper arms, shoulders and face were affected,
and the MD interfered slightly with his walk.

I wondered how he could possibly throw a ball
with accuracy or catch one thrown to him. The
nature of his affliction often created jerking motions,
uncontrolled movements of his arms and hands.
When Uncle Bill bought him his first baseman's
glove, he purchased, at my suggestion, a bigger glove
than usual which provided a wide area with more
catching space.

In the summer, almost every day, Bob and I would
"play catch." I would ask him to hold his glove palm
up as steady as possible and I would toss the ball, as
best I could, into the open glove. If my throw was on
target, the ball would often stay and Bob would
"make a catch." His return throws were somewhat
errant, but little by little they became more accurate.
Soon I was able to catch them without moving as
much as was necessary when we first began.

I don't recall how long it took, but each day his
catching got better. Soon he did not hold his glove
in a steady position as before, and was able to move
it into the path of the flying ball. He became adept
at playing catch. It was a joy to see him experience

something he had not been able to do for 25 years. He learned how to swing a bat and hit a thrown ball. We also practiced tennis and he became competent at hitting a tennis ball over the net.

"Coach Ray"

> *What may be lacked in talent can be made up with desire, hustle, attitude and a lot of hard work.*
>
> Don Zimmer

Early in life I discovered there is no better way to take your eyes off yourself or your troubles than to focus on helping others. My first team coaching position began at age 18 when I helped a group of 10 to 12-year old boys play little league baseball. I was also playing in a league and one of the fathers would assist if both teams had a game on the same night. The schedules were such that I only missed four little league games during a two-year period.

Occasionally, parents would ask that I give their son or daughter a little extra assistance. It was such a pleasure to see that child's skills improve. That was my reward. At our softball camp or during the City of Fairview program, there were kids who could not catch a ball or swing a bat properly, but they wanted to learn. They may never become big league All Stars, they may never play high school ball, but they can still play the game somewhere.

Coach Ray had quite a positive impact on my son in his elementary school years. David loved basketball and was an average basketball player. Most of the time he felt discouraged because he was given little playing time, even though he never missed a practice. After a game, he would throw his equipment into the car and say very little. Don Ray changed his outlook.

Coach Ray gave that something extra. He worked to develop not only the boys' basketball skills, but also their self-esteem. He made sure each boy had an opportunity to feel that he was a contributing member of the team. Basketball was fun again. Coach Ray set up a night when the boys got to play in a short game to demonstrate their skills during our high school games. The youngsters felt proud and important to be part of a high school activity with the "big kids." That night gave them the dream that if they worked hard enough, they could someday play on the real varsity team. We were blessed when David was placed on his team. For Don's rapport with the boys, his sense of humor, dependability, knowledge of needed skills and inexhaustible enthusiasm, we are grateful. Never did Coach Ray's diabetes become a factor in the boys' games. His perseverance through his "ailment" (no one ever heard him call it a "disease") was as deliberate as his desire to help the kids. We're not surprised that he is still coaching.

Joyce Hronek, mother and teacher

I dropped out of coaching little league baseball in 1953 and joined a local umpiring group. When not playing, I was "umping." I stayed with the Lakewood Umpires Association for five years and for the Parma, Ohio association for seven years. At the time of this writing, I have been working for the Suburban Umpires Association for nearly five years. In this way, although my playing days are over, I remain a part of the sport I love.

I coached and played for an adult basketball team in an under 6-foot league, and coached 3rd, 4th, 5th and 6th grade basketball for seven years, and little league football for two years. Most of my coaching endeavors were involved with baseball for high school boys and fast-pitch softball for girls. The opportunity to coach at this level was a rewarding experience, and I was honored to help these young men and women. By the way, probably 99% of the young people I have coached have no idea I am diabetic. Although I was on the verge once or twice, never did I have a reaction while coaching. I still had my juice jug near by, and made up my mind they would not see me have a wing-ding.

With my partner Bob Walton, one of the finest coaches I have ever known, we sponsored and coached a week-long clinic for fast pitch softball for thirteen years, from 1982 to 1995. The week-long camp was held in June and limited to 56 girls at each session. Young ladies between ages 13 and 18 came from distances of 75 miles to attend. We did not offer overnight stays and their parents had to find them lodging accommodations. Several of our girls gained All-American honors while attending college. Many of them received full college scholarships for their softball talents. The girls, for the most part, accomplished these achievements on their own, but we know for certain that we bolstered their spirits and boosted their skills.

Seven hundred kids, of both genders under the age of 15, came under my tutelage in '95 when I was named baseball director of Fairview Park. This had to be one of the highlights of my involvement with young folks. Many of these youngsters were in my elementary-grade basketball program from years earlier.

My responsibilities were to organize 48 individual teams by age and skills, so that one team would not be more talented than another, set up a schedule of 12 games for each, arrange for umpires, and use the six diamonds efficiently. Rescheduling "rainouts" was the biggest problem.

For me, it was all worth it.

More than once I have commented — about a life in the hereafter, or if I could return for a second life on earth — I would want to coach and teach young people, as best I can, the skills of baseball or fast pitch. In the 1989 film *Field of Dreams*, a ball field is built in Iowa and, magically, deceased baseball greats emerge from the corn field, ready to play ball. One of them asks Kevin Costner's character, "Is this heaven?" My answer would be, "Yes, a ball field is a place where reality mixes with fantasy and dreams can come true." The following illustrates just that.

James' Story

You should run on your own fuel;
it comes from within you — Paul Brown

One of the stories that will remain with me forever is when, nearly 50 years after I worked with Bob, I again had the chance to coach another individual stricken with Muscular Dystrophy. James' story is to me a significant one.

It was 1995 when 12 year-old James was signed up with the City program. The rules stated that each and every participant will play a minimum of three innings each game they are in attendance. This rule included James. His ailment was more affected than Bob's as his speech was more slurred, his walk or attempt to run was very awkward, as is characteristic of the disease, and his body movements, in general, were difficult for him to control. His youth worked against him as at age 12, he did not have the strength and acquired skills behind him to aid in competitive sports. But he had the desire — he had the "heart for the game."

The season was half over when I approached to see if I would be able to help this youngster. At this point he had batted 14 times and had been called out on strikes in each at bat. The team coach tried to place him in the field where he could do little harm. Regardless, his teammates always cheered and supported him, which was gratifying to see.

Lessons with James and me began slowly, carefully, as it was a trying task for him to catch a ball. My easy throws often struck him in the body or on the shoulder. It was just like when I helped Bob, only now much more difficult. We spent hours tossing and trying to catch. Each minute of each hour was torture as I felt that I might never be able to help this boy. He tried hard, he wanted to do this so very much. We continued. Eventually his coordination began to improve. Now his youth was in his favor. He became more controlled and every now and then he would catch a thrown ball. Along with his skill level, his confidence grew. He now acquired the ability to throw and catch, not as proficiently as his peers, but well enough to get by.

We turned our attention to his batting skills. James had not had a hit, nor had he touched a pitched ball during this or the previous season. The eye-hand coordination in hitting a baseball with a bat is difficult for everyone, and his coordination was extremely limited. A little league bat is 2 1/2 inches in diameter, while a baseball is a 9-inch circumference and approximately 3 inches in diameter. We have a 2 1/2-inch round bat attempting to hit a moving 3-inch round sphere. That is difficult! To hit a pitched ball, on what is referred to as "the sweet spot," it entails the exact center of the ball meeting the exact center of the bat. That space is an estimated 1/4 of an inch. Hitting a little lower than center creates a fly ball, while hitting slightly over creates a ground ball. Roger Maris, the first to reach 61 home runs in a Major League season stated, "One sixteenth of an inch is the difference between a fly ball and a home run."

I often think of Major League players. If they get 3 hits for every 10 batting attempts, they're .300 hitters. That is considered a good average and they earn millions of dollars yearly for hitting that percentage. That breaks down to 3 hits and 7 outs, which means they did *not* do the job 70% of the time. If I did my job only one-third of the time, I could not hold employment anywhere. Hitting a baseball is so difficult that this is considered especially great at the professional level where pitching is remarkably sophisticated. One of the best hitters of all time, Ted Williams, hit .400 one season. That meant he had outs 6 out of 10 tries.

Teaching someone without physical limitations to hit is an all-out effort. Building James' eye-hand coordination, reflex speed, vision skills, and teaching him to keep the bat level and on the same plane as the ball, and to time the swing to meet the ball was a wonderful task. Wonderful when it was completed!

As a training tool in coaching someone how to bat, I would mark a rectangular space (3 feet across and 5 feet high) on one of the many fences at the park, and would use that as our hitting target. We would position ourselves close to the fence and it would act as a backstop for the batted ball. All attempts were futile in the beginning with James, but we continued to work many hours. James could not hit a ball from a batting tee, he could not muster enough coordination to toss a ball in front of him and hit that ball with his bat. He could not hit one that I softly tossed in front of him. Again, this is always tough, but tougher for him. But tenacious James wanted to feel the thrill of hitting a baseball. I wanted this for him, as well.

We worked out after a 6:15 game; we worked out before a 7:30 game, and once a week his father would bring him to the park for extra practice. As each day brought us closer to our goal, my mood heightened. James began occasionally to hit a ball, first from the tee, then from my soft toss. But not, as yet, from his own toss. His confidence continued to grow. Each time he connected with the ball, his face would become a bright beaming light. My praise to him was endless, even if he only tipped the ball slightly.

As has always been my custom, I ended the last training session by going back to the hitting tee for a few ending swings. Then I would kneel down and place the ball on the tips of my fingers: I became the batting tee. The student was then requested to hit the ball from my finger perch. In each case, the novice players would pull back and express their fear that they would hit my hand. I assured them that there was no reason that would happen as I had utmost faith in their ability to hit the ball, not my hand. I have done this hundreds of times over the years, and my fingers received their share of hits, but never enough to do any damage. If it did sting, I would not let on, and let them know that they were swinging under the ball, and we would try again. It was most satisfying when they would knock that ball cleanly off my finger perch.

To be honest, I was leery to attempt this with James as he was not consistent. Because I was certain he had seen this done with other kids in the program, however, I did not want this to weigh on his mind. I knew I would end his training lessons with this exercise.

The last game of the season was at 7:30 that evening. James was there, long before I arrived. At 6:00 he was ready. He knew this was our last get together before his final game.

I followed my routine for the final session, but I omitted the hitting of his own toss. We took about one half hour. I then set the ball on my figure tips and challenged James to hit it as hard as he could. His face froze. He dropped his bat and almost as clear as a bell stated, "No, no, I'll hurt you." He was no different than so many others. I assured him that he could do it. I told him that he was now a proven hitter and he could smack that ball and not even brush my fingers. It took some prodding, but he slowly took his batting position. As always, he had a steady trembling in his stance. I could hear mumbling from onlookers: "That guy has to be nuts; that coach is soon going to be in pain." I do not believe James heard them as I was constantly talking to him. "You can do it — hit it on the button, right in the middle of the fence. Give it your best shot."

And he did. He hit that ball as cleanly from my fingertips as anyone ever had. The delighted look of surprise and the smile on his face were my reward. I praised him with everything I could think of to say, and told him, "You're ready now. Let's get out there and play ball."

As usual, James did not start the game. He sat on the bench, but this time he was the only extra. When his team was in the field, James was the only player in full uniform on the bench. His uniform was white with red trim and with red socks and cap. He cheered for his teammates. Once in awhile he would pick up a batter's bat. Once in awhile he would look around. I stayed out of sight but watched everything.

For me this was special. Here I was, a full-grown man who some fifty years earlier, when I was slightly younger than James, was told I could not, should not play baseball or any other sport. But I did play, and I was determined not to let this young man down. I attempted to put every bit of my baseball knowledge into this boy who, like me, also had an ailment. I wanted him to play ball even if perhaps someone told him he could not and never would. I couldn't wait for James to get into the game.

It was the beginning of the 5th inning and his team was losing by a count of 6 to 5. James took his position in right field. A ball was hit his way, but as usual another of his teammates fielded it. As the last inning began, another ball was hit toward James and it stopped rolling in front of him. He had trouble picking it up but once he got it in his hand, he made a decent throw to second base, and no runs were scored. From how he played earlier in the season to now, the difference was night and day.

And then, with a runner on first and second,

James had his chance to bat. He had not hit the ball all season — every at bat had been a strike out. I watched intently. The opposing pitchers were instructed to pitch carefully and softly to him as we certainly did not want him to be hurt. The first pitch was a strike because he merely stood there, as he had many times before. But on the second pitch, James hit it sharply over the second baseman's head and stood motionless in the batter's box. He trembled more than I had ever seen before. His teammates, his coach and everyone in the stands yelled for him to run. James didn't run, he lumbered; he began his journey to first base. The opposing outfielders had played him very shallow and his batted ball went between two fielders. James, to the screams and cheers of his teammates and the crowd, was slowly closing the gap between himself and first base. He shuffled, he lunged, but he got to first base and stood there with the most joyous expression any of us had ever seen. I had never been more thrilled on a ball field — I thought I would explode with excitement.

But there was more to come. The pure picture of satisfaction came when each and every teammate rushed onto the field and hugged, leaped upon, high-fived and knocked James down in their exuberance. The runner that scored the tying run also was part of their delight. The second runner had only reached third base, but he too joined in this mass of joyously unbridled youth celebrating James' accomplishment. I do not believe that James comprehended at that moment that he had fielded a ball, hit a ball, run successfully to first base, and drove a runner home. But he did know that he hit the ball. He had hit the ball! And to James at that moment, nothing else mattered.

When peace was restored, the boys took their places back at the bench area, the runner returned to third base and James attempted to wipe the infield dust from his uniform. This was his first pleasurable experience at having a dirty uniform! On the next pitch, it skipped past the catcher and the winning run scored from third base. They won the game. But more importantly, James had achieved his goal. He hit the ball!

I never saw this young man again after that evening. Often I would see many of the kids around town at a local store or a movie theater but never again did I see James. Wherever he might be, whatever he might be doing, I know that he has found success. He would settle for nothing less.

The unfolding of that triumphant event was marvelous. Nothing like it has ever occurred again in my lifetime, yet this once was enough. It has put a very large smile on my heart and etched an unforgettable picture in my mind. That smile and memory will last as long as I live. Thank you, James.

Umpire

Recently added to our Suburban Umpire schedule is the Catholic Elementary School girls' fast-pitch softball. The 5th and 6th grade girls of the CYO League are just now learning the sport. For this reason, we are asked not only to umpire, but to help them with the fundamentals of the game and their skills. To be able to coach and also call balls, strikes, safes and outs is a complete package for me. Occasionally, I will stay after a game with the coach's permission to lend individual attention to a student.

The worst thing I ever hear on a ball field is

parents yelling at their kids. Children and teenagers need encouragement and positive feedback, not name-calling and other negatives. The nicest thing I hear on a ball field these days is "Nice game, Ump."

Managing sports is like managing diabetes

My parents taught me how to manage my diabetes and, in turn, manage my life. Through this process, I needed the positive and negative consequences that life provides. I needed a pat on the back, I needed to be pushed on occasion, I needed a kick in the backside, as in 1948, and I needed care and attention. The "atta boy" and "way to go" were freely given when called for, as was the scold or constructive reprimand.

Between my parents and the manager I had at age 17, I learned to juggle many important factors, prioritize, keep records and statistics, and do what I felt was right. Other coaches and mentors in my work career provided that I never stopped learning. I came to realize that managing in the workplace and on the ball diamond does not differ very much. It comes down to paying attention to people, respecting their differences and treating them individually. There is an old expression that reminds us "no two people are alike." Even though some may have similar traits, some people respond to a challenge, some need the occasional push, some need to be "babied," some need recognition and some encouragement.

In managing my diabetes, I learned discipline. Whether I am managing a ball team, a department in corporate America or my life with diabetes, there is benefit to being conscientious, thorough, organized and alert. My family reminds me I'm efficient at keeping notes and reminders — this, too, came from managing my diabetes.

From the time I first managed a baseball team to managing a lifetime of diabetes, I have discovered that I like it. There is reward in "being on top of your game, " whatever game that may be.

I *have known Don for close to 50 years. We worked for the same company and played amateur ball together. Don is a man with many "hats" which include motivator, leader, coach, athlete and family man. He is dedicated to all his roles.*

To share three stories that come to mind, one combines his role as motivator and his life as a diabetic.

Don was the manager/player of our softball team that won the Cleveland Industrial Championship, which entitled us to play in the nationals in Charlotte, NC. Through various means, Don spear-headed a drive to raise money to pay for the entire team's airfare, food and hotel bills. Before one of the games, Don called the team together for a pep talk before we took the field. The opposing team's first batter hit a ball deep into left field and Don ran right through a 3 1/2 foot snow fence trying to catch the ball. He was not hurt but that driving desire to succeed has always been there despite, at times, running low on sugar.

The second story touches me to this day. My job was relocated to Kentucky and Don and I would talk by phone a few times each month. On one occasion, I mentioned that I was in a bad batting slump and our team was going into a major tournament. On the following Saturday, my doorbell rang and there, to my amazement, was Don. He had driven eight hours to pitch batting practice to me and to watch my swing. After hitting for a couple of hours and lunch, Don started the eight-hour trek back to Cleveland. His help ended my slump!

Last but not least, my secretary's teenage son was diagnosed with diabetes. She had taken him to two doctors and came to work shaken and crying. I told her about Don and placed a call so that they could talk. Not only did he enlighten and assure her that her son could lead a normal life, he offered to visit her son at any time. Again, a 16-hour round trip. This lady told me numerous times that Don eased and comforted her far more than the physicians.

Jeb Weidrick
friend and former teammate

I was fortunate, for 22 years, to have a part-time job at Rube Adler Sporting Goods. I first met Mr. Adler when, as a teenager, I entered his store to find my first ball glove. He let me try them all on for size because he knew that picking a ball glove was as important as choosing a second skin. When I found the right glove, I asked him to keep it on "lay away," that I would pay for it over time. I turned to leave the store. "Don't you want your glove?" he asked me. He knew I needed and wanted this glove, and he trusted I would be back to pay in full. I took my glove and from that time forward, I would cross town to buy my sporting goods at Rube Adler's. It is there I met Jim Mayer, who now owns his own sporting goods dealership.

The Man Who Showed Me How

How would I have made it in business if it were not for the watchful eyes of my buddy DR? As a young rookie starting at Rube Adler's, I was introduced to a part-time employee, a gentleman named Don Ray. It was a joy to work with a seasoned veteran like DR. He showed me the ins and outs of the sporting goods industry, which he knew so well because he used most of the equipment.

The day started with Don coming to the store, maybe a few minutes late because he was bringing fresh, warm, still-dripping glazed doughnuts from Becker's Doughnuts. Then, after showing me how to sell product along with handling the customer (the DR way of never being short on words, explanations and hand gestures,) it was time to replenish our energies with lunch from Alesci's.

A well-planned deli menu of half a pound of this and half a pound of that, ended up with about five different meats and cheeses on fresh Italian bread. Interestingly, Don was the doughnut and lunch courier, but I don't recall him ever eating one of those doughnuts, or having more than a normal meal. I worked with Don for months before I learned that he was diabetic. I learned to give him a sugar "fix" when he needed it, and get him back to the man we knew best.

Don knew how to treat the customer to perfection. Always a detailed explanation on the reason why that product should be bought. Don, as many know, is a stickler for details and neatness. The heat seal machine was Don's baby. When a logo or number was applied, it was put on with *precision — with Don it was PERFECTION, and it still is today. It is a quality he acquired by taking fastidious care of the measurements and weights associated with his diabetes.*

Today, the rookie (that's me) has become a seasoned veteran. In more than 20 years of owning Jim Mayer Sporting Goods, my good buddy is still telling me and showing me how to do the heat seal machine. In Don's eyes, I'm still learning. He is still telling me the logo and numbers are not straight enough. That's my man DR. I appreciate everything he taught me.

Jim Mayer

9
Winding Down

Take time from doing to enjoy being. Anonymous

TIME

To realize the value of one year,
  ask the student that has failed a class.
To realize the value of one month
  ask the mother that gave birth to a premature baby.
To realize the value of one week,
  ask the editor of a weekly newspaper.
To realize the value of one hour.
  ask the lovers that are waiting to meet.
To realize the value of one minute,
  ask the person who missed the plane.
To realize the value of one second,
  ask the person who just avoided an accident.
To realize the value of one millisecond,
  ask the Olympian who just won a silver medal.
Treasure every moment that you have.
  Yesterday is history — Tomorrow is a mystery.
Today is a gift.
  That is why they call it the "present."

Anonymous

For most events in life, we prepare. We warm up, so to speak. Before a baseball game, we "wind up," we loosen and flex our muscles to get "stretched out." After a game, there is a cooling off period, muscles are again slowly stretched. After a big event in life, most of us take time to unwind, to settle down after much excitement. So it is for me. I'm now in the process of winding down in both my athletic and professional careers.

In my mid-40s, I began to look at things differently. I decided that I would continue playing softball, with some basketball in the winter. That worked well for many years as I also branched out into umpiring and coaching. By the time I was age 50, I already had three knee operations and my job couldn't afford my being out of commission. In addition, I needed to devote more time to my family as the children were growing up all too fast. My football playing went from regular tackle to touch tackle. (However, I believe that game can be more brutal than the tackle version because we wear no pads. And although we didn't tackle, we would often dive at the ball carrier to make a "tag;" still, a tackle would somehow find its way into the contest.)

When, at 52, the age at which both my father and my good friend Howard Ferguson died, I was nowhere close to dying, but I realized my ball playing days were over. There comes a time when all of us need to stop doing something that we love. For me, it was baseball, and I told my teammates and coach/manager that my last game was to be that season. Though I never had a pinch runner, not even at 52, my speed wasn't what it once was and in general my skills had diminished. Overall, my defensive abilities had slipped. I could still hit, but then, in slow-pitch softball, the pitching is similar to pitching at a picnic, so my carrying a .600 batting average was no big deal.

At the last game, the guys prompted me to close out my career with a 4 for 4 night. That's 4 hits in 4 attempts. I smiled and nodded that I would try to do so. Each inning of the game, that thought stayed in my mind. My first at bat brought my first hit, my second at bat produced another, and my third attempt was a sharp single. I was now 3 for 3. My teammates were wild with enthusiasm when I came to bat for what would be my last time.

I stepped into the batter's box and probably received another one of those thrills that you store away in your heart. Every player in our dugout was cheering, every guy was pulling for me to get that last hit, to go out 4 for 4. I can still feel that moment as I am writing these few sentences. I hit one of the pitches as hard as I could hit a ball and it went directly at the shortstop. I put my head down and raced, flew down that first base line, realizing I had just hit my last pitch. Even though I knew this would be an "easy out," I may have run faster that evening than at any other time of my playing career. I had never "dogged" it before and would not do so now. I made an out in my last trip to the plate, but that's okay. Those young guys who will now take over my position, will, hopefully, run every hit ball as if it might be their last at bat. They will give it their ALL and see that the reward is in the playing of the game, itself.

Yes, I made that one out, but I recall even more the feeling of the wind pushing against my face on my way to first base, and I can hear it racing past my ears. That's the feeling and the sound that describes so much of what baseball is to me.

Although I decided it was time for me to call it quits, it was at this point that I delved into coaching and umpiring to fill the void that not playing would leave.

I have been fortunate. In addition to participating in ball games all my life, I was able to play two years of semi-pro football, have an invitational try-out with the Philadelphia Phillies, and play baseball in

Cleveland's Municipal Stadium on two different occasions being cheered by over 50,000 people in attendance. I had the opportunity to play in two national tournaments: one in baseball and one in softball. I was chosen Manager of the Year by the City of Cleveland for leading our team to a State title, and played in a World Championship in Charlotte, North Carolina. I was nominated to the Softball Hall of Fame for the City of Cleveland, but that honor has eluded me. I am, however, very proud to be have been nominated.

My wing-ding with "the Pros"

During my last year of competition in the Premiere Major Softball Division, I had the good fortune to play and room at out-of-town games with a former member of the NFL's Cleveland Browns. This became my last year with one of the nationally-ranked teams in the country, Sheffield Bronze. At one of the out-of-state tournament games, I had a dandy of a reaction. It frightened Sanford Gross, the owner and coach, so much that he let me go at the end of that season. As he explained, "I don't think I could go through one of those again. You scared the hell out of me." However, he offered me an assistant coaching position and wanted me to remain part of the team, but I still had the desire to continue playing. That was in 1967. I was 33 years old. I played for another 20 years but never at that level.

The wing-ding that made such an impression went something like this: I roomed with Preston Powell, a second-team fullback with the Browns. He was the backup to Jim Brown, one of, if not THE finest running backs that the game has ever seen. I have watched pro football for over 50 years, have been a Browns season ticket holder nearly 44 years, and have watched many great running backs. My opinion is that Jim Brown was the best there was.

In any event, we lost that first game on Friday night. That made it difficult at a tournament of this magnitude, as when you lost one game, the schedule always was geared to have a losing team eliminated. They piled game after game on us and it was generally extremely tough to win a tournament when you lost that early. On Saturday, we were scheduled to play five games, the first at 9:00 AM and, as I recall, the last at 8:00 PM, a feat for anyone, never mind a diabetic.

When Saturday arrived, I took my morning shot at a reasonable hour and ate a decent breakfast. We grabbed lunch "on the run," and dinner, if you can call two hot dogs, fries and an orange drink a dinner. I kept my juice jug filled with whatever I could get at a food stand, and I always added sugar to the orange or lemonade drink. These games were not played in one location, and buses transported us from field to field.

A slow-pitch game usually lasted 90 minutes or less. We never had too much time between games to relax. In the four years I played with Sheffield Bronze, we had, on several occasions, played three games in a day, but never five! Imagine playing five hard-fought baseball games in one day! This doesn't happen often but it is a "load" when it appears on the schedule. Because we won all the games that day, we were 5 and 1 at that point in the tournament. We were all as dirty as coal soot and were all physically beat. I played every inning and my eating and insulin-taking were off schedule and, in short, all messed up. Between playing and traveling, we were out there for nine hours.

Coach Gross was visibly happy, however, that we were still in the tournament. He wanted everyone to clean up and have a relaxing dinner at a fine restaurant across the road from our motel. I knew that this would help me get my meal-planning regime back on track. Preston and I were all for eating and hurried to our room to get ready.

Many of the guys, as well as Sanford, knew I was diabetic, but none had ever witnessed an insulin reaction. Preston was one of the players that did not know. He showered while I lay on the bed, covered only with a towel. I fell asleep and drifted into a wing-ding. When Preston came out of the shower, he had no idea why I didn't respond to his attempt to wake me. He noticed that I was soaking wet. He didn't know what to do, and, said later that I frightened him to death.

He called for help and apparently most of the other players came into the room because I could hear many voices, though I couldn't reply. I heard one voice say, "He needs sugar." Another voice said, "He needs one of his insulin shots." Several voices chimed in and argued as to whether I needed sugar or a shot. Finally Sanford ordered that they call for an ambulance.

I was taken to a local hospital where they catheterized me to get a urine test. That, by the way, is not pleasant. The test registered a very low 58. They fed me intravenously with a glucose solution and I gradually became aware of my surroundings. I sat up on the gurney where I had been placed, covered with a hospital sheet. I looked about and it appeared the entire team was outside the window, looking in. I gave them a nod, a wave and they all motioned back. The nurses insisted that I remain quiet for a few more minutes and I did so. They continued to talk with me and agreed that I was okay.

I thanked them, apologized for putting them through this, and tossed the sheet aside. I was stark naked. I grabbed the sheet to cover myself as quickly as I could and stepped down from the table. The team, though, thought it was quite funny. For me, it was more embarrassing than the "no shirt" incident at Ohio U.

Diabetes, our constant companion. Our mighty and powerful companion. If we neglect to take care of it for a day or portion thereof, it reminds us of its presence. To neglect or ignore our diabetes is like ignoring a dropped fly ball — you can do it, but not if you want to stay in the game.

Impotence

It's nice to be important, but it's more important to be nice. Anonymous

I include the phrase above as the doctor, after his examination, stated that I was impotent. At first I thought he said that I was important.

With age, we humans "wind down" sexually, as well, but I'm including this chapter to let other diabetics, specifically the men, and their families know that with advances in medicine, sexual abilities may diminish or disappear but it does not need to be a problem.

I had reached the middle of my 57th year on this

good earth when I started to notice that I didn't have that usual early morning penile erection as frequently as before. I also noticed that it was becoming more difficult to generate an erection during those pleasurable moments of sexual intimacy. More noticeably, when an erection was established, it was short lived.

I believe I read somewhere that one of the most feared or unwelcome things in a man's life would be the inability to generate an erection. From adolescence we associate penile erections with physical manhood and psychologically this "failure" to perform could trigger for some thoughts that masculinity is somehow failing. At any rate, it was a difficult "pill" for me to swallow.

Fortunately, today's medicines are right on target, and the condition is not difficult to deal with, should a diabetic choose to deal with it. Today, with Viagra, Muse, the vacuum pump and other medical aids, it becomes a non-issue. We can continue to enjoy intimate relationships with our partner. In fact, it might even work out better than before!

The examination was fairly simple; various tests were performed, fancy equipment was used to determine whatever the doctors were looking for. The bottom line was that I wasn't getting the proper blood flow into the penis and the prescribed medicine took care of that. Sometimes the ease, or convenience isn't there, as it is necessary to take a short leave of your love nest to get the needed medicine. Often, if preplanning can be arranged, you need not leave your mate to get that "helper" at all.

In a number of doctor visits I had about this, they stated that I was fortunate to be experiencing this situation at age 57. That many young men, even in their early twenties and thirties, have experienced the same condition. Men of all ages are touched by this, but it is quite prevalent in the life of a male diabetic. They informed me that having kept my sugar in good control throughout my life made it possible for me to keep my body in good shape in many ways, including sexually. Doctors have been impressed by the physical condition that "this diabetic" is in. I recall one physician I met in August, 1998. He was interviewing me but never looked up from his notes until he asked my age. When I answered, he realized I had had diabetes for over 60 years. Finally, he looked up from the form, put down his pen, threw his left arm around the back of his chair and said, dumbfounded, "No kidding?" He continued to look me straight in the eye for the rest of the interview and seemed to take a sincere interest in my case. We must have talked for an hour.

Years and years ago, when I was first learning the ins and outs of Sugar Diabetes, I decided that the thing to do was to take care of myself by following the diabetic rules: watch my food intake, keep it in balance with the prescribed insulin dosage, check my sugar levels at least three times a day, stay away from sugary foods, and live a happy life. I never thought at that time how important all this was going to be later in my life. It turned out to be the critical factor in my health. I'm sure, without the attention I gave the rules, my health would have suffered and I would not have accomplished nearly as much as I have.

The care that I've taken certainly helped save my life, literally, just a few years ago, after a major car accident.

10
Car Accident

Never drive faster than your guardian angel can fly.

Anonymous

A car accident on June 30, 1998, nearly took my life. My family has mixed emotions about whether my blood sugar level had anything to do with this major incident, or if it was just one of those things that happens. I place the blame on my poor judgment.

It was near the end of the work day when I was driving west on a six-lane highway, heading home. I decided to make one more sales call, at one of my customer stores. As it turned out, that was a choice I wish I could reverse. My decision turned into a tragedy that occasionally still haunts me.

I passed the exit that would take me home and headed toward the tentative appointment I had with my customer. We had arranged that if I could not see him today, I would see him the next day. It was only 4:00 and I knew I could make that stop and still be home by 5:30. The rush-hour traffic was becoming heavier, and as happens regularly, road construction was on-going. Every now and then we commuters would come across those orange barrels helter-skelterly lined along the highway. I remember thinking that I was in the wrong business: I should have invented orange barrels for road construction.

Traveling at speeds of 68 to 70 miles per hour in the center lane, I found myself behind a slow-moving automobile, traveling much slower than most of the traffic. The posted speed limit was 65 MPH. There was solid traffic in the lane to my left but fewer cars in the right lane. I waited for an opportunity to pass the car. An opening appeared to the right, a little tight, but enough to make a pass. There was a semi-truck in that lane but it was a good distance ahead of the car that I was about to pass. A good 50 yards ahead — plenty of room for me to pass and still be well behind the truck to make my re-entry into the center lane. The car behind, in the right lane, was to the rear possibly four or five car lengths. I put the car into its passing gear and made my move, keeping close watch in my mirror of the oncoming vehicle. All seemed fine and I would be around the slow car in seconds. My attention was then devoted to the space ahead and almost instantly, the truck's tail lights came on. The truck seemed to stop at once. I too went to my brakes but I was rapidly approaching the truck. The next sound was almost deafening — the shrill scream of the truck air brakes. I pushed as hard as I could on my anti-lock brakes, but I had nowhere to go, no where to turn, it happened so suddenly. I just couldn't stop. I hit the now-motionless truck with such a force that I couldn't then, nor can I now, express or describe the hit, the power, the force of that impact. It was tremendous.

I recently saw a film, *Angel Eyes*, starring Jennifer Lopez as a policewoman wherein a truck accident takes place. It honestly took my breath away. Even though it was several years after my collision, the scene brought tears to my eyes. It was just a quick, brief glimpse, but it might give an idea of the force, and an experience of this tragedy.

The State Troopers, by using skid marks and other means, judged that my car was traveling at 57 MPH when I hit the truck. One of the troopers indicated that if my 1996 four-door Oldsmobile had been smaller and lighter, my injuries might have been much worse. Without seat belts and without air bags, it was suggested that I probably would not have made it at all. If the troopers mentioned the seat belt and the air bag once, they mentioned them a dozen times. A phrase I heard time and time again, "good thing you had your seat belt on, good thing you had air bags." I'm sure they were right. One trooper commented, "I've never unbuckled a dead man." The "Olds" was a leased car in good condition with low mileage, and I had planned to purchase it when the lease was over. Interesting, the lease was to expire on July 10, only ten days away. There was no way anyone would want that car now; it was "totaled."

When the powder from the air bag settled, and the steam from the radiator water disappeared, I looked around and realized I was still alive and that I was in much pain. I have experienced pain before but never like that day. I did not lose consciousness and was able to talk to concerned people that had gathered, to the truck driver who apologized repeatedly, and then to the emergency paramedics and the State Troopers. The steering wheel was tightly pressed against my chest, my legs were somehow wrapped up under the dashboard and both my chest and legs hurt like hell.

Blood was everywhere, most noticeably in a

puddle on my lap that was created by the "cup" formed by the zipper in my trousers. I was drenched in blood; it still fascinates me that I needed just 7 stitches to close the only severe cut I had. That was on my right hand. I had many small lacerations all over my chest, face and arms. Flying windshield glass caused small cuts that did not need much attention but certainly created a lot of blood.

The dashboard was pushed toward the rear of the car, an automobile that had measured 20 feet in length. It now probably did not reach 14 feet from front to back, and resembled a large, partially open accordion. I kept a plastic 14" x 24" box in my trunk that contained record folders of my customers. This container weighed about 25 pounds. My rear seats had back rests that could be unhooked and dropped down if extra space was needed. Lengthy items such as wood lengths or rain gutters could be carried in the trunk and then placed through the seat opening. The record container was now beside me, balancing on the dashboard and the passenger front seat. My first reaction was, "What the heck is that doing here?" The container had "blown" through the back seat and knocked off the passenger seat head rest. My car phone had jumped from its cradle and lay in my lap, partially in the blood puddle.

I had planned to go out to dinner that night to celebrate a belated Father's Day with my wife and Dawn and Dave. After I became a little more oriented, I picked up the cell phone and called Penny to tell her that it was doubtful that we could go out to dinner that night. I was very calm as I did not want her to know the severity of this mishap. When she asked why, I then told her that I had a car accident and had to go to a hospital for x-rays. I told her I thought my leg was broken but no more details.

The EMS vehicle arrived and since I had no idea where they were to take me, I handed the phone to one of the emergency team who told Penny they would take me to Elyria Hospital, seven miles away. She double-checked with them to make certain they understood I was diabetic.

The EMS personnel were repeatedly concerned about my neck and I kept telling them that it was okay. They evidently didn't think so, or it was a precaution, but they strapped a brace to my head, neck and upper back and told me not to move, to sit still. Believe me, that was easy to do; every slight move meant more pain. Still, I managed to see some humor because I really couldn't move much anyway.

They worked as a team and everyone seemed to have a definite job to do. Two people were dabbing blood from here and there. One of the female team members, in yellow garb, was on her back, on what was once the car floor, underneath me and the steering column, attempting to free my legs. As she worked, she talked to me, assuring me that everything would be all right; she told me that she would have me "unstuck" and out of there in "just a few minutes." I don't know how long it took, but it seemed like hours. Every now and then she would call to me, smile and give me a little wink. I, of course, winked back.

Her presence was a refreshing breeze! However, each time she moved one of my legs, the pain jabbed like a lightening bolt. Finally my legs were free. I couldn't move them but when asked, I could wiggle my toes on both feet. She remained in that prone position for quite awhile, bracing my legs until they could prepare a "prop" to hold them. They removed the door, spread the door opening wider with a powerful, mechanical device, and gingerly, very carefully, removed me from the car in almost the same position I was seated. There were about five paramedics carrying me and constantly asking, "Are you all right?" I continued to reply, "Yes." Certainly, along with checking on my physical condition, they were attempting to keep me conscious and mentally alert.

When we got to the gurney, with several hands supporting my entire body, they placed a brace on my back from below my spine to up and over the neck brace. They repeated that I would be fine and that they would get me to the hospital in a short time. They then began to move me to the center of the gurney and when they laid my body down, it was a horrid "wake up" call because the pain, now worse than before, shook my whole body. When they attempted to lower my legs, it was so obviously unpleasant that they placed pillows under my legs, and in a few minutes I was resting as comfortably as I possibly could under those conditions.

The truck driver kindly stayed with me until the EMS van left. He apologized several times and let me know that a construction truck had backed into the highway, causing him to use his air brakes. The State Troopers, the people that stopped to help, the EMS personnel, all were very caring. I thank each of you. To the driver, in the gold and blue nylon jacket and dark blue baseball cap, who was so concerned, I want to let him know that I'm okay and all is well. Thanks for staying with me.

Once inside the EMS van, many tests were begun and I was hooked up to most of the available equipment. I told them that I was diabetic and naturally they tested my sugar level. They reported it was 82. I expressed that those numbers were incorrect. I felt my level was not that low because I had complete control of all of my faculties, mentally and physically, as well as being aware and alert. I also knew I had eaten a well-balanced, filling lunch a few hours before.

One of the crew replied that they were having some problems with that monitor and they were to have it checked. I suggested that they do that as quickly as possible since their reading was not even close to being accurate. They did not give me anything by mouth but one of the devices inserted into my arms may have carried a glucose solution. When we arrived at the hospital, I was hooked up to various machines and I insisted that I have another test on my sugar level. They did and the results were 187, a long way from 82.

This part of the accident is still a subject of conversation in our family. I am positive that an insulin reaction, a wing-ding, did not play a part in this. That my sugar level was 187 is evidence that I was not having a wing-ding. My wife contends that my sugar level was "up" because of the intravenous glucose I received in the ambulance; she believes I was having a reaction at the time of the crash. Immediately after the incident, I thought so, too, but in retrospect, I do not believe that was the case. Here is why:

I have had hundreds, thousands of insulin reactions over the years and in each case they were very similar but each had a touch of their own mystery about them. Some have been more severe than others. For me to have been in a "state" where I could lose control of a car or run into a truck, I would need to be in a very serious reaction. Even if the 82 were correct, it is not low enough to put me into a reaction that severe. In extreme reactions, my body coordination and muscle control is poor, and my speech is slurred or I have no speech at all. During the incident and after, I did things I would not have been able to do had I been having a wing-ding. I would not have been able to turn off the car, call Penny on the cell phone or make tongue-in-cheek comments about our dinner plans. I would not have been able to answer every question asked of me by the troopers and joke with the EMS personnel or wink at the female paramedic.

The collision was caused because a construction truck had backed into the highway, forcing the semi-truck to brake, and the fact I was attempting to pass and possibly did not allow myself enough space. I was to blame for poor judgment. All this entered the picture of this event that greatly impacted our lives.

At the time of this writing, I am still in sales with Roman, Inc. distributors of fine giftware and collectibles such as Seraphim Classics Angels and Fontanini figures. I continue to travel by car, ever mindful of the extra diligence I must give to driving and to traffic.

Not long after I arrived, Penny joined me at the hospital. Even with a 30-mile trip, she arrived, as always, to be by my side.

They did all that they could do at this small city hospital and due to the way our hospitalization programs worked, I could not stay there, anyway. They were extremely competent at this emergency room, but before midnight I was flown via helicopter to a hospital on Cleveland's east side. The thought of a helicopter ride threw fear into my heart as I knew a situation had to be critical for a helicopter to be called into service. Yes, I felt bad, but was a helicopter really necessary? When I questioned this, they were emphatic that the "air" ride was needed. Maybe I was worse than I thought.

The original intention was to fly me to Cleveland Clinic but they had no available rooms, and so the flight took me to a neighboring hospital, Mt. Sinai. I remained there from Tuesday until Friday afternoon. On July 3, 1998, I spent my 64th birthday in Mt. Sinai, the same hospital where I was born.

On that Friday morning, I lost consciousness. I passed out as I was leaving the lavatory returning to the bed. Penny and an attendant at the door both heard my body hit the floor. I dropped straight down. I felt the collapse coming but could do nothing about it. This was a first, and a unique sensation. That afternoon I was taken to Cleveland Clinic, five miles away, and placed in the Intensive Care ward where I remained for three weeks. Thanks to the nurses and doctors at Mt. Sinai, you were lifesavers.

My injuries: nine broken ribs, a collapsed lung, a bleeding liver, a shattered right leg with damage to the knee, the left leg was twisted and sprained at the ankle and knee, severe blood clots developed in both legs and I had other minor internal injuries. Because of the clots, filters were placed surgically (and still remain) in both legs to capture those little rascals as they break apart and travel up the blood stream in my legs. The physicians, nurses and aides at Cleveland Clinic were extraordinary. They did all they could and then some. Percentages of my coming out of this were slim although none of the family ever shared those thoughts with me. Months later I learned from a friend that he was told I had a 50/50 chance to pull through. One of the complications was that I could have "drowned" on the blood seeping from my liver.

*D*on *had been in the hospital for several days but his condition was worsening. I had medical training and as an honorary family member, I visited him and reviewed his charts. He looked bad. On paper he looked worse. Recovery was a distant thought; survival more imminent. Blood clots, liver lacerations and swelling were severe. Questions existed as to whether the proper blood flow could be rejuvenated. He was in bad shape. During surgery and the various tests, Penny never left his side. Obviously worn out, she believed in his strength, his will to live and God's blessings that had been bestowed thus far. When rehabilitation finally began, Don would never accept the doctors' remarks that he might "have to live with it," relating to the tremendous edema, swelling of his lower limbs and the limited use of his legs. He would not accept that as the final answer. His recovery is miraculous and to see him living, and I mean LIVING, is a joy.*

Mary Lynn Marsh, Nurse Practitioner

The treatment I received was continuous around the clock, every minute of every day. One incident stands out in my mind and reveals how dedicated the nurses were: It seemed that I could not get anything cold enough to drink; no matter how much ice, no matter how much the nurses stirred or shook the water container, nothing was cold enough. I did not want to eat and a cold drink of water was about all I wanted. (This thirst for cold water continued for several months after the accident.) My diet and insulin were all fouled up because my food intake was miserable, and insulin was injected as needed. The nurse assisting me asked if I would like a Popsicle? Wow, did that sound good — can't get much colder than that and it would have some flavor. She checked with the doctor (there is sugar in a Popsicle) and he agreed that it would be fine. What flavor I would prefer? I answered "red or orange." She apologetically returned with grape. I told her it was all right, that grape would be fine. Within the next several minutes, another of the nurses who had been busy at the foot of my bed, approached with a brown paper sack. Contained in that sack were red and orange Popsicles, saying that she got them from another ward that would never miss them.

I came home on August 1 to a hospital bed in the family room of our tri-level house. I could not walk, I could not sit up, I needed a bedpan. I could not concentrate, not even to watch a ball game on TV. I had difficulty staying awake, eating was a rare event. We made Popsicles with unsweetened Kool-Aid but, all in all, I wasn't having any good days. A day nurse came every day for a month, did various tests and generally stayed for 30 minutes or so. Gerri and her husband Jack McTigue came from Florida and stayed with us. I don't know what we would have done without them. Once again, Gerri was watching out for her "little" brother. We brothers-in-law bonded for life as Jack helped me in ways that only brother can help brother. My daughters and sons-in-law were here often to lend a hand, even though Dawn's new baby Mitchell was not even one year old, and Sheila, having just given birth to twins, was pregnant with Evan, her fourth child. Debby gave birth to daughter Emily on July 2 in Mansfield, Ohio, two days after the crash. Penny attended the birth, with her love for her family carrying her the 100 miles between hospitals. Scott was in Europe at the time, along with my sister Donna and her French husband, Michel.

My eating was almost nonexistent as the desire to eat just wasn't there. I still enjoyed that cold drink and a Popsicle but hunger never came. We had a heck of a time trying to adjust my insulin intake to the small amounts of food. This was a concern for everyone but Penny handled this most touchy situation. Penny was my Angel throughout this entire ordeal. Without her, I don't know if my recovery would have turned out as well as it did. She has always been my Angel but her "wings" were so evident during this time of our lives.

Soup for Body and Soul

Generally soup served during the hot month of August is an unusual selection, but when, during my second week at home, Penny asked if I could eat some of her homemade potato soup, it sounded perfect. An excellent cook, Penny makes a marvelous soup, with potato soup one of my favorites. I know that I smiled as I replied, "Yes."

Hours later she served a bowl of piping hot, totally irresistible potato soup that only she can do. It was the most tasteful, most delicious thing I had ever eaten. This was a far cry from the cravings for ice cold, but it was probably the one thing that got me on the road to recovery. I ate and then ate some more. The huge kettle she always uses to make the soup took up two burners on the stove, and I believe I ate the entire contents in the next several days. The nutrition began to give me strength, and with it I became more alert and more mobile. I started to watch television and baseball again. More, the soup was a gift from someone who cared. That soup was the best medicine I could have had.

Penny insists that Scott's return from Europe also had a lot to do with my recovery.

Scott's Homecoming

When news of my automobile collision reached Scott in Europe, it was an intentionally watered-down version of the crash. Penny and I did not want to panic him or my "kid" sister, and we did not want to interfere with Scott's plans to live in Spain for the summer as part of his international studies. When Scott telephoned home, he was told I had a "fender bender." Scott continued with his trip to Toledo, Spain, while I remained in the hospital.

I sure missed him, and at the same time I did not want him to see me in my pitiful condition. The closer Scott came to returning home, the more determined I was to be in good shape, as good as possible, to welcome my son home. When he returned from Europe in mid-August, I was in the hospital bed in our family room, on oxygen, plugged with needles, and legs elevated. In general, I still looked pretty bad. When he saw me, his eyes filled with tears. So did mine. His tears were tears due mainly to the way I looked; mine were because it was pure joy to see him! He would only be home for three days before he had to report to college football practice. He spent almost that entire three-day period right there with me.

The morning of his departure, when his teammate and driving buddy arrived, Scott helped me sit up in bed, hugged me gently but firmly, and then stated that he was going to dedicate this last football season to me. I jokingly replied, "I thought you dedicated every season to me." We both laughed at that and then he said, "This is my last year; it's going to be special and I am going to put your name on every yard I gain." We again said good-bye, hugged, and he left.

His final season opened the second Saturday of September. In the past I had never missed his pre-season practice games, never mind the season opener but my doctor said firmly that I could not go. I could argue all I wanted but "no" was his answer. Penny agreed. The doctor advised that I might need to realize that I may not be able to travel for another month. "Wait until October to see how you're doing," was his advice. I, on the other hand, told Penny there was no way I would miss the opener, only 16 days away.

Penny, who also loves to watch Scott play, might be his second biggest fan. Maybe it's a tie. At any rate, she finally relented and said that if I could continue to improve, we would go. In the next two weeks, I did everything I was asked. The day nurse and the physical therapist were pleased with my progress. I was not going to miss a game. Penny knew that, too.

Game day came. Penny fixed a special pillow for my head, as it was necessary for me to ride with my legs raised. My head rested on this pillow which rested on the back door window. She also rigged pillows and rubber pads to put under my legs so that they would be somewhat elevated. It is about a two and one-half hour ride one way and a three-hour game. Since I was directed to keep my legs elevated every hour of every day, this was going to be a difficult eight hours. I did the best I could keeping my legs higher than my head, as instructed and, thanks solely to the efforts of "PennyRay," a name I use lovingly as a nickname, we got there. I wondered if truckers passing by asked, "What the heck is that in the back seat?"

We settled into our usual seats at the stadium and immediately looked for our Scott Ray, #34. I could not see a # 34, but noticed a player walking very much like my son, built a lot like my son, walking directly toward the stands, appearing to look directly at both Penny and me. This player was not wearing #34, however. When he reached the sideline, he removed his helmet. It was Scott. He held his helmet aloft, touched his hand to his heart, then to his lips and threw a kiss to us. He then pumped his helmet up and down and pointed to the numbers on his jersey and blew another kiss. The number on his jersey was a brilliant white on red. It was #37, my former football number. He paid me the highest tribute possible from one player to another on a ball field. Often players will carry another player's numbers on a card in their pocket or, as a further honor, wear an old, numbered jersey of a former teammate as an undershirt. But to trade his own special number for mine, to go to the trouble of having the team make the switch . . . . I have never been at once so startled, honored and touched before in my life.

Recovery

I attempted to return to work by making sales calls on the telephone from home but I really needed to get back on the road to see my store owners and buyers. Besides, most of them were friends by now and I wanted them to see I was walking and working. In September, Donna, back from Europe, traveled from her home in Phoenix to see for herself that I was on the road to recovery. She acted as chauffeur as I began visiting clients.

Until mid-November when I got the go-ahead, I was unable to drive. Then, I was frightened to sit behind the steering wheel. To regain my confidence, I backed up and pulled forward in our driveway for several days. I drove around the block a few times to get the rust off and to re-acquaint myself with driving. Before Thanksgiving, I was back on the road, having been away for 4 1/2 months. Although I wasn't completely back to normal, I was headed in the right direction.

A Note About This Accident

These following sentences are directed especially to my diabetic companions. Taking care of our diabetes is important because it can save our lives in a completely different arena. Taking care of diabetes can save you not only from the harmful effects of diabetes, but from, for example, an automobile crash, as well. Evidently, that is what happened to me. On three different occasions, three different doctors said to me, with a family member in attendance: "If you were not in such good condition, if your diabetes was out of control, if you had not been physically active, or if you were excessively over weight, if you had smoked or had high blood pressure, it would have been a great deal more difficult and complicated in getting you well." One even added, "... if we could have saved you at all." From the earlier medical comments that I may not ever walk again or to the 50/50 chance to make it, I believe the three doctors, (orthopedic, vascular and internal medicine) were right. I was in good shape for a 64-year old guy, my sugar levels were consistently checked and were normal, and I did eat the right foods — my diabetes was in control. Take care of your sugar diabetes, take care of yourself, it can help you in ways you cannot anticipate or imagine.

Reflecting on the events that prompted this chapter, my humble thanks go to the good Lord above as He not only helped me through this trying moment in my life but also allowed me not to hurt anyone else. I only hurt myself! What if? What if I would have collided with a family of five just leaving on vacation, what if I had run into a school bus, what if someone had been in the automobile with me, and I had hurt someone else, what if I would have killed someone? I am so very blessed that these "what ifs" did not happen. That is another reason that brought tears to my eyes at the movie theater: tears of happiness that no one else was injured.

I was fortunate in many ways, but to have only hurt myself was another blessing God let me have.

11
You Can Handle It

Tough times will pass, tough people go on and on.
Abraham Lincoln

Diabetes "Dust"

When I am asked to speak to groups of diabetics, especially to audiences of children, the story I tell unfolds like this, —

In 1939 I was almost five years of age, of normal size, blond curly hair (that is now as straight as a poker, but fortunately still there), and as active as any other kid my age.

At about that very same time, God was looking down through the clouds for a very special person. He was searching for a youngster that looked as if he or she could handle most anything. The reason for this search was that God held in his hand a container of Sugar Dust, droplets of Diabetes that are so small they are almost dust. I believe that God chose me, and at a specific time, sprinkled that sugar dust down through the clouds. I don't know the exact time these sprinkles showered around me but it must have been near the time my family and I moved to Pennsylvania. The exact day doesn't really matter. He chose me and therefore it couldn't be all bad. God had a feeling that I would be able to handle

Sugar Diabetes. He was right. I did handle it for many years. You can, too!

If you received this sugar dust it's all right. It just makes you sweeter! Diabetes is a special challenge, and everyone is given a challenge. Some people's "challenges" are harder to live with than diabetes. Diabetes is not a sickness like the cold or a flu; it is a way of life. To live with it, you just follow the simple rules. Know that you are the "boss" of your own life, but your doctor is your foreman or supervisor. He or she has many valuable ideas and suggestions on how to manage your special Challenge. Find a doctor knowledgeable in sugar diabetes and then listen to him or her. Doctors always have us "sugar employees" in mind with each and every decision.

Follow this advice and you will lead a healthy and happy life. By the way, when God sprinkles Sugar Dust on you, He also includes sprinkles of "do not get sick very often" dust for as long as you take care of your diabetes. While we wait and hope for a cure, we still must meet our Sugar Challenge every day.

Good Health

> *Whatever you are doing in the game of life, give it all you have. Don't be a "holdout."* Anonymous

It is true that when God decided to sprinkle the "sugar dust" on me, I also received "good health dust," and have been fortunate in other areas of my health. I don't believe I have been ill more than twenty times in the many years that I have been in this wonderful world. I can use the adjective "wonderful" as it has been that for me. Good health has been one of the reasons. I doubt my wife could come up with more than six times in our forty plus years together that I have been ill.

I can count on one hand the number of headaches I've had, and on two hands, the amount of aspirin I have taken. When I was ailing with the flu, a sore throat, an upset stomach or bad cough, it was rarely harsh enough to keep me home from work. At American Greetings Corp., there was an incentive package that gave employees cash bonuses for not exceeding the five days allowed yearly for excused sick leave. For 12 consecutive years, I received the cash award. Because the five sick-day leave could be transferred to vacation days, I extended my vacation to three weeks instead of two each year. Also offered was a small reward for non-tardy employees. I received this bonus ten out of 12 years. It wasn't the monetary award that intrigued me; it was that I just didn't get sick.

I never missed playing in a baseball or football game due to illness. However, the year I received a flu shot, I got the flu so severely I thought I was going to die! I missed two basketball games. It was the first year I'd taken a flu shot, perhaps in 1978 or '79, and it was my last.

I've had a few sports injuries over the years, and three knee operations. I lost part of my ring finger when, at six years old, Sis accidentally slammed the car door on my hand. My hip bone was fractured when I tripped while washing the car in spring, 2000. The days I spent in the hospital were not because I was sick, but because of broken bones or diabetes. I don't refer to diabetes as a sickness. My pancreas may be sick, but I can live and work with that! Again, I think of diabetes as a way of life; it is certainly the way of my life.

Good health can, indeed, accompany diabetes. The health I have been blessed with is, I believe, due to good luck and to the care I have given my diabetes over the years. Again, I eat my allotted food and it is generally food that provides nourishment. I drink no alcoholic beverages, I avoid junk food and desserts, attempt to stay in shape and watch my weight.

Taking care of ourselves is paramount, and the advances in research and medicine are making it much easier.

12

We've Come a Long Way:
A Diabetic's Perspective

*Courage is not how a man stands or falls
but how he gets back up.* Anonymous

The care and treatment of Type 1 Diabetes have come a long way. The means of testing blood sugar, the methods of monitoring at home, the various insulin types available, the tablets and "the pump," all help to control high sugar levels. Now, diet is regulated by size of portion, rather than by weight, and through meal planning. If one's sugar level is under control, and to aid in controlling it, exercise is usually recommended. When I was a kid, I wasn't supposed to move!

Testing for Sugar

When it was discovered I was a diabetic, the only home test for sugar level was by checking urine, usually three times daily.

Sixty plus years ago and for many years thereafter, we tested our sugar levels by urinating into a container. Then, using an eyedropper we would deposit eight drops of urine into a test tube, add six drops of water and then finish this mixture with eight drops of Benedict Solution. (Benedict Solution was the same solution I used, because of its dark blue color, to deceive my mother prior to my coma.)

After this mixture was slightly shaken to thoroughly mix the ingredients, the test tube was placed in a pan of boiling water for three minutes. To hold the hot tube, we used a special metal "gripper." We would again give the test tube a little shake and the resulting color would determine my blood sugar level. If the color remained dark blue, my sugar level would be, as a chart would verify, "negative" or no sugar of any consequence. If the color was an aqua shade, it meant a slight trace of sugar was present. A distinct green shade would determine I was a 1+ which meant between 150 and 200. The higher the figure, the higher the sugar content in my system. If the color became yellowish brown, I was a 2+ which signified I was at a 200 to 250 level. A color of brown would place me in a 3+ category and my count was in the 300-350 range, much too high. The worst color for us to see was reddish brown and that classified me at 4+, meaning above 400. Before the coma, I was testing 4+, or possibly a rating, unknown at the time, of 5+.

For many years I visited a hospital once a week to have my blood count evaluated by the hospital staff. This was along with daily home urine tests. All of this is so primitive compared to our present methods that it is hard to believe.

This is how it was done: A nurse used a very sharp, flat (not round) hypodermic needle and would jab a hole in one of my fingertips. Once the blood was prompted from the fingertip, it was drawn into an 8-inch long, slender glass tube. To draw the blood into the glass tube, a rubber tubular attachment was placed at one end. The other was placed into the nurse's mouth. She (or he) would actually draw the blood into the tube by sucking the rubber conduit as if it were a straw. The glass tube would fill about an inch or so, and then the nurse would pinch, or crimp, the rubber so that the blood would not seep out, hold a gauze to the open end of the glass tube and very quickly remove the rubber part of this contraption. She would place her finger over the upper end of the tube, again so that the blood would not escape, and then deposit a few drops of blood onto a small, rectangular glass palate and would then insert it into a machine for the final testing phase. This was done once a week for the first ten years of my diabetic life, and later it was done in a doctor's office. This practice continued until the availability of the home-use glucometer.

Daily routine tests for sugar levels are still required, but now there is modern equipment to make things easier and for convenience during travel. Glucometer test strips and various hand-held appliances poke tiny holes in fingers and draw blood. Inserting the test strip into the meter gives an instant and accurate record of sugar count. In the future, the need to prick a finger may disappear as devices are appearing on the market that seem to "read" through the skin.

Insulin Then and Now

My first insulin prescription was for Protamine Zinc and Regular. I believe those were the only two that were available to us. This was 1939 and insulin had been discovered and produced in the mid-to-late 1920s.

A Canadian physician, Sir Frederick Banting received the Nobel Prize for Medicine for his discovery of insulin. He shared this honor with Dr. Charles Best. (Doctor Banting died in 1941 in an airplane crash.) The Protamine was a slow-acting insulin that carried throughout the day, while the Regular insulin began much faster and would be at full strength within 60 - 90 minutes. There are other insulins available to us today: intermediate-acting insulin NPH and Lente, and quick-acting Humalog used to help manage sugar when eating or when blood sugar is out of control. Regular is often prescribed as the insulin-of-choice today.

When they were first introduced and marketed, I tried the "tablets" for less than a week. My sugar level became so out of whack that it took almost another week to get my sugar back to an acceptable state. The tablets were just not for me. I have since learned that a Type 1 diabetic should never be given tablets at all! Tablets are to enhance insulin that exists in the system, as is the case with Type 2 diabetics. Type 1 diabetics do not produce insulin at all or certainly not enough to be worthy of enhancement. This is the case of a physician not recognizing the different treatments necessary for Type 1 and Type 2 diabetes, evidence, once again, that the patient, the diabetic, must be ever vigilant.

I'm told that some physicians today recommend that the urine be checked for other chemicals besides sugar, for example "ketones." Ketones apparently signal that control of the sugar level may be at risk of going out of control. (See *Diabetes 101* found in the Information and Referral section.)

The Era of the Glass Syringe

Forty years of my diabetes management included use of a glass syringe, rather than the plastic syringe we are accustomed to now. From 1939 to 1980, I used a glass syringe with a removable sterling silver needle. (I still have the honing stone I have used since 1939 to sharpen needles.) With each injection, morning, noon or evening, we were required to take the plunger from the outer part of the syringe and place both parts into a cooking pan. We also placed the silver needle in the pan and added an inch of water. We would then boil the water for several minutes to remove any and all germs. When I took two shots, we did this twice a day. If three shots, we boiled these three parts each time. We would then carefully pour the water from the pan, and place the three parts of the syringe together. Caution was used to avoid touching any of the parts that came into direct contact with the insulin or the needle's pointed end that would soon be placed in either my upper leg, upper arm, stomach or buttocks. Ouch, I really disliked the shots in my derriere but I took so many shots that I had to find "fresh" parts of my body to stick with that sharp needle. A black and blue mark would rarely appear on an arm or leg.

When taking two shots in a row (of two different kinds of insulin), we would not re-boil after one of the injections, rather, we would wipe the needle with a swab soaked with Isopropyl alcohol. Then I would draw the proper dosage of the second insulin and inject it into the alternate leg or arm. I have not used my buttocks or stomach for many years for an injection, except during my hospital stay following the car accident. For 25 years, when my dosage called for two different insulin types, I took two separate injections. Then, when I was about 30 years old, I discovered by talking to another diabetic that I could mix the two, taking only one shot. When I first heard this, it was at one of my "talks" to some fellow diabetics. I almost argued with him about this and thought he was entirely wrong. My doctor confirmed the next day that he was correct and was surprised I was not aware of it. It was one of those take-it-for-granted situations. I began mixing that very day. I calculate that I have 9,000 extra holes in my arms and legs!

Just as the glass syringe era was ending, I began to place the syringe in a test tube that was filled, to cover the needle, with the Isopropyl alcohol. This would keep the needle free from contamination and the glass injector did not need to be boiled several times a day. When the plastic syringes entered the marketplace, they were preferable because they were disposable; however, I have kept the same treatment going, and I also put the plastic syringe in a test tube with alcohol. In this way I use them for more than one injection. Some medical professionals may not approve of this method of sterilization, but it was originally recommended to me by Doctor Roenigk. My test tube stands erect in a drinking glass, held in its upright position by a handful of plastic wrap surrounding the tube within that glass. It works for me!

Dosage and Me

For most of my life I took two shots a day, a shot in the morning before breakfast, and a second at dinner. For a short time, I took three shots a day:

morning before breakfast, noon before lunch and 6:00 before dinner. I took them at the same time every day with routinely scheduled meals, as recommended. The injection in the morning was generally two types: Protamine Zinc and Regular, or Lente and Regular. In the evening I took one shot and it was of the Regular insulin. For the past 15 years, I have taken NPH along with the Regular in the morning. Recently, in the past year or so, I have been taking Humalog in place of the Regular. The Humalog seems to be okay, but sometimes I think the Regular was doing a better job. It's about even. My long habit with Regular makes me lean toward it, but I want to wait and see to give Humalog a fair chance. New types of insulin are on the horizon.

At the beginning it was trial and error getting the sugar levels and the insulin to be on "the same page." As years went by, and I grew and became more active, the insulin and food again needed balancing. As my size and weight increased, so did my diet. We approached the new food quantities with a unit more or a unit less of insulin, based on the calories I was consuming. The process of adjustment and balance continues today; as my diet varies, so does my insulin intake.

Heredity

Several years ago, the theory emerged that Type 1 diabetes is triggered by a virus in individuals predisposed to it. I understand that many diabetics and medical professionals today subscribe to that theory. We also hear from knowledgeable medical people and diabetics that diabetes is hereditary, handed down from grandparent to parent, from parent to child and you're that child. Yes, in many cases that certainly is true. Still, some of us with sugar diabetes are the first in a family. I have always believed that it has to start somewhere and for most diabetics, it is not a genetic hand-me-down. Science now tells us 90% of Type 1 diabetics have no family history!

I was born in 1934 and there was no record of diabetes in our family. Dad was 32 years old when I was conceived, and I was three years old when it was discovered that Dad's mother, my grandmother LeNora, at age 59, was diagnosed with adult-onset (Type 2) diabetes. Dad was born when LeNora was 24 years of age and it was 35 years later that she was diagnosed with diabetes.

I have always asked myself these questions: How could Dad have inherited the Type 1 diabetic gene, juvenile diabetes, when his parents or grandparents didn't have diabetes when he was born? Was my dad a carrier for 32 years and passed it along to me? Neither of my sisters and none of my known cousins have diabetes. The way I have dealt with the answers to these questions is to believe it was just my turn to be one of the chosen. I believe that my children, all four of them, did not have diabetes because the sperm I produced was healthy and not affected by prolonged abuse of sugar, or any abuse of liquor or alcohol, when each of them was conceived. Apparently research has shown that alcohol affects sperm, why not sugar? According to US News & World Report (June 25, 2001), babies born to mothers with gestational diabetes during pregnancy are also prone to juvenile diabetes, again reflecting the importance of the parent's health on the unborn child. I believe my children did not inherit the "gene" because I did not inherit it. My beliefs have held true: my kids are now between the ages of 25 and over forty and none of them or my grandchildren show any diabetic tendencies. Maybe it will appear later, but it has not shown itself yet.

I did not have access to recent theories as I was living my life. Nor could I wait for explanations. Those of us who have had diabetes for half a century have had to carve our own path. I only know that my thoughts and the things I did "worked" for me in helping me lead a "clean life." This "clean living," non-abuse of sugar and alcohol, has only benefited my family and me. Diet and lifestyle can allow us to lead healthy lives.

Research

According to the Juvenile Diabetes Research Foundation, we know that someone is diagnosed with juvenile, Type 1, diabetes in America every hour. We know it can and does strike adults, up to age 40, with the average age of diagnosis at age ten. We also know that children can get Type 2 diabetes, usually tied to obesity. We know diabetes is on the rise. Science tells us that diabetes is an "autoimmune disease." I dare not begin to deal with these subjects. I'm a practicing diabetic, not a physician. Referrals to sources of information on diabetes are available at the end of this chapter.

The ongoing research and improvements have been remarkable for diabetics. The future holds more tremendous results. Just watch and see!

Statistics

I've always liked to keep score, keep records and make statistical comparisons, not only about athlete's scores and "stats," but about other areas of life. One of my favorite stories is about the difference between a million and a billion. If you were to receive $1,000 a day for three years, you would receive a bit more than $1 million. That's $365,000 per year. If, however, you were to have a billion dollars in a three year period, you would need to receive $1 million dollars each day. That is one tremendous difference.

In many ways, the society in which we live has gone from a million to a billion. A few years ago it was reported that nearly 4 billion (billion not million) pounds of candy were consumed yearly in the United States. That averages 18 pounds of candy per person. Someone must be eating a lot more because I don't eat any! (If I do, it's because it is medicine, a sugary fix that I need at once.) In my youth, candy wasn't as available as it is now. We would be fortunate to find a grocery store or a drug store within a five-mile radius of home. In the city today, we have grocery stores every few blocks and convenience stores in between. Full-scale drug stores often are found next door to grocery stores. Not only can you find a store, but you can choose your favorite store to shop for sale items. Restaurants and delicatessens, too, are everywhere. In all these locations, candy and soft drinks are offered. I'm told the top selling item in drug stores is candy. No wonder they pack it in row upon row by the check-out counter where marketing wizards on Madison Avenue have determined it will sell best. For me, sweets and soda pop are a special indulgence, and taken only when needed.

Today, children in America consume soft drinks daily, along with potato chips and snacks, all pure carbohydrates. Not so around the rest of the world, not so when we were kids, and certainly not so in our household.

The abundance of consumed "carbs" now correlates to the increase of diabetes in young and old. It is no surprise to me that the incidence of Type 2 diabetes, which is linked to weight and obesity, is rapidly on the rise. All the insulin pumps in the world will not be able to replace common sense and healthful habits.

A Lifetime of Stats

The truest disability in life is a bad attitude.

Scott Hamilton, Olympic gold medalist and cancer survivor

At one time I rationalized that if I averaged one wing-ding a week, that would be 52 per year. So, of the 365 days in a year, 313 of them did not involve a reaction. That's 86%. I have been a diabetic for about 23,000 days. Using this average, I have had a wing-ding 3,200 times in 63 years. They are not to be looked at lightly, but there were 19,800 days as normal as any person without diabetes. In addition, a wing-ding generally lasts only minutes, not days. If we broke this down into minutes per year, I had millions of minutes where I was as healthy as any other man.

To relate to a batting average, I would be getting a base hit 86% of the time and making an out only 14% of that career. Not bad. I wish I could have done half that well when I played baseball. That's an .860 batting average.

Those 3,200 days were significant; they, along with my daily practice of taking insulin, were the outward signs of my condition, the signs that my family and friends witnessed. To those around me who helped, who provided the sugar "pick me ups," it might seem as if there were many more insulin reactions. Especially to Penny as she encountered more of them than anyone. One theory holds that while I was dependent on insulin all my life, Penny was "co-dependent" on it. She has been my partner in my diabetes, my co-diabetic. I hope it was not too hard on her, but sometimes I know it was.

Sure, each of us with diabetes is going to have some down time, but, fellow diabetics, do not ever let it get you down. Diabetes may not be completely beaten yet, but, thankfully researchers are working on that. One day in the not-too-distant future, the research foundations and others working toward a cure will have the diabetes so well controlled it won't even make the top 25 in "cause of death."

In the meantime, we sure can have our winning time far outweigh our losing time. I'm beyond my 67th birthday, and I am still in the game. Not only am I still on the playing field, but I'm still in the game of life. Precious life. My goal is 87 years of age. Set your sights on that top number. I'll plan to meet you there.

A Note to Young Diabetics

No one can make you feel inferior
without your consent." Anonymous

I find when looking back, a pleasure and a disappointment that I experienced while in elementary school.

The disappointment I experienced was because of my doctor's "order." I could not participate in sports or exercise in any way. During gym class, I would take a seat on a folding chair and watch my classmates play various games. I knew inside myself that I could also compete in whatever game they might be playing. When we had the chance to go outside, to recess or to gym class, I could only stand and watch. No swinging, no slide board, no running or playing tag, just sit on the stone steps and watch. It felt very sad.

The pleasure was that although my classmates could have used this as a reason to "pick on me," they never did. I was the only diabetic in our school, but nobody ever teased me about diabetes. Instead, they seemed interested in what diabetes was, and that anyone could get it. Maybe they learned to care about the ailment and respect it because I did.

Often we hear that some children can be very mean, even cruel, when it comes to their peers. You may hear of a situation where a 6th grader or a "bigger kid" picked on, teased or tried to embarrass a classmate. You may even have experienced this yourself. Rude kids and "bullies" exist. Sometimes we can't make them stop and we need help from adults to deal with them. Their actions are wrong and have no place in school, on the playground or anywhere else.

If I could relive a time in my life, it would be those years in school. If that time of my life were mine today, with the advanced knowledge that is ours about diabetes, I could play kick ball, slide on a slide and play tag with the best of them. I could have even strapped on roller skates and skated to school if I chose to do so. I could not do it, but I hope that is what you do now. Even if you lose a limb to amputation, I hope you play and run. If someone does say something unkind or negative to you, I hope you will be flying so fast and be so happy about your life that their words will bounce off you just from your sheer speed, energy and self-confidence.

The expression at the start of this section reads, "No one can make you feel inferior without your consent." That means, no one can make you feel bad, unless you let them. If it were me, I would not feel bad because I would be playing, running and leaping, as happy as a flying bird!

If you are ever the target of a bully, or someone's verbal abuse, please remember this comment. It is a statement my dad always shared with me in reference to life in general. Now I want to share it with you, my youthful diabetic teammates — keep this with you always:

"You are as good as some,
but you're better than most."

Heading for home

If you are not willing to walk away, win.

W. Donald Ray

My diabetes has never been too heavy or burdensome for me to carry. I carried it like an emblem on my sleeve, the number 5 or 37 on my jerseys. It was my Ozark Ike bat or the mask on my football helmet. I have played the game of diabetes for, so far, 63 innings. It has been a contest in life that covered the past 63 of my nearly 68 years of life. Those years, those "innings" were unique as each one presented a challenge to me that I would not give in to. The diabetes batted in the first half of each inning but I have had the last at bat. Once in a while the diabetes would score, but I always came back to at least even the count. As I look back over those years, I believe I outscored diabetes by plenty. I will be so bold to say that it outscored me twice, at age five and at age 14, but the rest of the game was mine.

And each pitch was unique, like a fast ball, a curve, a slider. The pitches thrown to me by the Diabetes team were diet, injections and insulin reactions. I learned how to step up to the plate and how to adjust to each pitch. In my innings in life, I sure did learn how to hit the "curves" thrown to me.

There is nothing more exciting in baseball than an inside-the-park home run. Here, the ball is not hit over the park fence, but stays within the confines of the baseball field. It is a ball that is playable, able to be fielded by the opposition. Diabetes has been like that for me. It never left my life completely, but has remained in my life's arena. My eye has always been fixed on it. My offensive and defensive skills were focused on winning. The challenge was there. I accepted it, I ran with it, and I strove never to let it get ahead of me or my team.

With an inside-the-park home run, there will almost always be a play at home plate, and it will usually be a close call. I knew, as a runner rounding third base and heading for home, that the fielder would make his throw to home plate and the ball, the catcher and I would reach the plate at the same time, within fractions of seconds.

The excitement of living with diabetes for over six decades is the same excitement or thrill as rounding third base beating that inside-the-park challenge. To score, I had to beat the "tag" by the catcher. To outscore diabetes, I have needed to respect its constant presence in my life, to be ready for a challenge by staying alert to a "big play," a major reaction or a complication wanting to "beat" me.

Diabetes may have scored once or twice, but he never beat me. He never did and he never will. A tremendous "will to win" helps make that slide into home plate, it drives our legs a bit more to get around the bases faster. Our desire to score is what makes diabetes so much like a baseball game. Diabetes often tries to beat you but you just don't let it without giving it all you've got, and then some. My desire to win was such that when it tried to beat me, as when recovering from my car accident, I just wouldn't let it. I know the consequences if I had "given in." I know that if I had not been playing "good ball," the outcome would have been different. That accident was the toughest "curve ball" I ever had to hit.

You, my diabetic partner, my teammate, can also take the last at bat for the many "innings" of your life. Do your best by playing fundamentally sound, and by following the rules of this game of diabetes. You just keep doing the right things to outplay the diabetes team. In this way, you are ready to take advantage of any "luck" that presents itself to you. Acknowledge that you have the best team made up of doctors, family and friends. Importantly, the team captain is YOU. You provide the motivation and the leadership. You can win.

And you are winning as long as you are still in the game.

Afterword

My name is Katie Roenigk and I am the great-granddaughter of the Dr. Roenigk in this story. I was given Don Ray's manuscript to read by my grandfather because many chapters are about a teenager's life and he thought I would relate to it. In it, I also found a man's philosophy of life: to take what was given to him and make the best of it. He didn't let his illness bring him down in any way, and instead, used it to make a difference in the lives of other people. I've never met Donald Ray, but I can tell that he has touched many lives with his love for teaching, his skill at coaching and his excitement about baseball. His diabetes didn't seem to affect what he accomplished in his daily life at all. In fact, nearly all of the kids he coached didn't know that he had a disease unless he told them.

To my great-grandfather, Dr. Henry H. Roenigk Sr., young Donald was a patient, someone who needed care. Don Ray now speaks warmly of Dr. Roenigk, who passed away in 1986 after suffering a stroke in the late 1970s and Lou Gehrig's disease. To hear the compliments and praise given to him makes me proud, especially as I contemplate a career in medicine myself. In these pages, Dr. Roenigk is spoken of as if he could fix anything. He would often show up, if momentarily, and Don's family would think that "the problem is under control, Dr. Roenigk is here." He saw the patient as a whole person and passed that concept on to my grandfather who shares his name and went on to become a physician, as did my father. My father and granddad are both also professors. Dad is chairman of Dermatology at Mayo Clinic in Rochester.

Throughout the book, Don Ray's attitude is shown to help "fix anything" and turn a problem around. There are two separate stories in this book of young men with muscular dystrophy that Don coached through sports to show that no matter what their shortcomings, they could still do their best, improve, strive for their goals and feel proud. It shows that you don't need to be an all-star if you love "the game," whatever your game is, with all your heart.

I've learned that living with diabetes takes discipline. I can't imagine going through my teenage life without being able to eat or drink whatever I want. That Don couldn't play high school sports would have angered me if I was put in his shoes. He was obviously able to play since he played for other organizations, yet he wasn't allowed to represent his school until his senior year. This seems close to a tragedy to me, knowing that he probably had more heart than most of the others on the team. His love for sports overwhelms me. I would give anything to sit out at gym class some days! But Donald Ray kept himself disciplined and ready to make the most of his life. For him, being told "no" made him strive even harder.

"Still in the Game" can mean many things at the same time. It says that you're still in the game even if you aren't the center of attention. It can also mean that you're still able to hit the ball out of the field and slide into home. It can mean that being part of what you love is a privilege to honor for as long as you can. Or, ultimately, it can mean that you're still alive and loving life.

I am motivated by this philosophy.

Katie Roenigk
Great-granddaughter of Henry H. Roenigk, Sr.

Diabetic Dietary Myths

Myth #1   *If you have diabetes, you should never eat sweets or sugar again!* The American Diabetes Association states that sweets can fit into the meal plan as long as they are counted as part of the day's total carbohydrates.

Myth #2   *Never drink orange juice.* One-half cup orange juice can fit into any meal plan. A higher fiber choice would be a fresh orange and therefore more filling.

Myth #3   *I will have to prepare special food for myself and different food for my family.* The meal plan for diabetes is a healthy eating plan for everyone. No special food is needed to purchase. Watching portion sizes and counting carbohydrate foods are the key.

Myth #4   *I can eat unlimited foods that are labeled sugar free like sugar free pie and sugar free ice cream.* Sugar free does not mean calorie free. Check labels as these products still contain carbohydrates and need to be counted in the meal plan.

Myth #5   *If I take diabetic medication, I do not need to worry about what I eat.* A regular eating schedule and carbohydrate counting are essential in order for your medication to work best.

Myth #6   *I always look at the sugars on the food label to determine if it is okay to eat.* It is best to focus on the Total Carbohydrates on the food label because some foods have natural sugar and cannot be avoided.

Myth #7   *I should avoid all pasta, bread and potatoes.* You need carbohydrate foods for your body to function. The goal is to eat the right amount of carbohydrate foods.

Myth #8   *I can never eat out again!* Most restaurants serve huge portions of food. Just watching the portion size can decrease the amount of calories and carbohydrates. Take home leftovers!

Myth #9   *It is okay to eat only one meal.* Remember to avoid slowing your metabolism and blood sugars, eat some breakfast to start your body running.

Forget the "good" food and "bad" food idea, and just eat healthy !

by Karen Dunn and Jill Barsa
Registered and Licensed Dietitians
Fairview Park Hospital
Cleveland, Ohio

Fact Sheet — Type 1 (Juvenile) Diabetes
presented by the Juvenile Diabetes Research Foundation

More than one million Americans have Type 1 (juvenile) diabetes — a disease which strikes children suddenly, makes them insulin dependent for life, and carries the constant threat of devastating complications. Someone is diagnosed with Type 1 diabetes every hour. It can and does strike adults, as well. In Type 1 diabetes, a person's pancreas produces little or no insulin, a hormone necessary to sustain life. Although the causes are not entirely known, scientists believe the body's own immune system attacks and destroys insulin-producing cells in the pancreas.

The Truth About Type 1 Diabetes

It Affects Young Children: It's one of the most costly, chronic diseases of childhood and one you never outgrow.

Insulin does not cure it: While insulin allows a person to stay alive, it does not cure diabetes, nor does it prevent its devastating effects: kidney failure, blindness, nerve damage, amputations, heart attack and stroke.

Diabetes needs constant attention: to stay alive, those with Type 1 diabetes must take multiple insulin injections daily and test their blood sugar by pricking their fingers for blood six or more times per day. While trying to balance insulin injections with their amount of food intake, people with Type 1 diabetes must constantly be prepared for potential hypoglycemic (low blood sugar) and hyperglycemic (high blood sugar) reactions, which can be life threatening.

Diabetes is difficult to manage: Despite rigorous attention to maintaining a healthy diet, exercise regimen and always injecting the proper amount of insulin, many other factors can adversely affect a person's blood-sugar control including: stress, hormonal changes, periods of growth, physical activity, medications, illness/infection and fatigue.

Statistics and Warning Signs

Even with insulin, Type 1 usually results in a drastic reduction in quality of life and shortens the average life span by 15 years. Each year approximately 30,000 Americans are diagnosed with Type 1, over 13,000 of whom are children — that's 35 children each and every day.

Warning signs of Type 1 diabetes include: extreme thirst, frequent urination, drowsiness or lethargy, increased appetite, sudden weight loss for no reason, sudden vision changes, sugar in the urine, fruity odor on the breath, heavy or labored breathing, stupor or unconsciousness. These may occur suddenly.

Information and Referral

For information on Type 1 juvenile diabetes, contact your state office of the Juvenile Diabetes Research Foundation (JDRF) — or

Juvenile Diabetes Research Foundation International
dedicated to finding a cure
120 Wall Street, New York, NY 10005
(212) 785-9500 or 1-800-533-2873
(9AM - 5PM eastern standard time)
www.jdrf.org

For information on Type 1 or Type 2 diabetes, contact:
American Diabetes Association
research and advocacy
1701 N. Beauregard Street, Alexander, VA 22311
1-800-342-2383 (Monday through Friday 8AM - 8PM)

The Diabetes Exercise and Sports Association (DESA)
1-800-898-3372
www.diabetes-exercise.org

Suggested reading:

Diabetes 101, A Pure and Simple Guide for People Who Use Insulin by Betty Page Brackenridge, and Richard O. Dolinar, M.D.

Don W. Ray can be reached by e-mail at donwray37@aol.com

Index

Ignoring your diabetes is like ignoring a dropped fly ball. You can do it, but not if you want to remain in the game.

DWR